# RESOURCE DEVELOPMENT

## GOING TO THE NEXT LEVEL

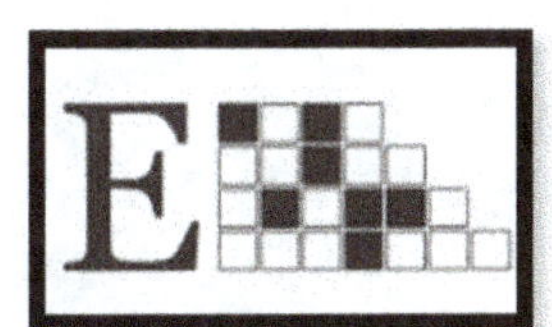

## Eurydice Moore, M.A., Ph.D.

www.mcclurepublishing.com

## DISCLAIMER

THIS BOOK PROJECT WAS MADE POSSIBLE THROUGH FUNDING BY:

A partnership with the Chicago Housing Authority (CHA) & Housing Urban Development (HUD)'s Section 3 BUSINESS CONCERN COMPETITIVE GRANT

This book is dedicated to my
daughter Rita Nashell McClendon.

# ACKNOWLEDGEMENTS

### Anna White

I dedicate this book in memory of my maternal great-grandmother Anna White. She showed me charity by taking me in at three months of age. My great-grandmother was known as Big Mama in the community. She fed people and housed people that were at a disadvantage in life during her generation. Anna even raised other people that were non-related to her. Upon her death, over 3,000 people attended her wake at standing room only. People were out the door at the funeral to pay tribute to my amazement, and many announced she helped them. It is because of her, I have a charitable heart. She was my introduction to charitable work also known as Not-For-Profit. She did not have an official organization, but she had the heart and fortitude to serve. I salute you, Anna.

### Doreen Mormans from Mormans Consulting

I dedicate this book to you as well. You bailed me out of a difficult situation and were very instrumental in assisting me to obtain a business grant to update and upgrade my skills so that I would better serve my clients. I will never forget your labor of love.

### God

Always and forever!!! It's because of You that I live, move and have my being. You made it all possible to publish four books. This is miraculous. It's divine.

# INTRODUCTION

This book will cover three main topics, which I hope will be helpful to you the reader.  The book is comprised of three divisions which are as follows:

**Division I - Not-for-Profit Business (NFP)**
**Division II - Resource Development**
**Division III - Funding and Grant Writing**

The Not-for-Profit division gives information regarding how to set up a Not-for-Profit such as incorporation, the 501c3 determination status, and focus on the business side of the Not-for-Profit, which includes the various governmental entities that you must have contact with such as your Secretary of State, Department of Revenue, Attorney General's Office, and the Internal Revenue Service.

The resource development division is the NEXT step once an organization has been incorporated and has obtained the 501c3 determination.  It is in this section that grassroots fundraising and frugal campaign activities are given as examples in acquiring resources for the organization.

The last division explains funding and grant writing which provides information on various fundraising projects, and explains the LI's purpose as well as how to write it and a Standard Grant Proposal. This division has a sample Letter of Intent, along with a Standard Grant Proposal to serve as a guide to jump start you in funding and grant writing.

This book is mainly for start-up Not-For-Profit businesses and could also benefit those Not-for-Profits that have been in existence for a while in some capacity.

# Table of Contents

## DIVISION I - NFP Incorporation

After over thirty (30) years of experience in Not-For-Profit ("NFP") also referred to as Nonprofit ("NP") and Non-Governmental Organizations, this book was written with you in mind. Surprisingly, majority of my work experience has been associated with some type of NFP.

My first job was a high school student working for the summer in the mayor's youth program. The minimum age to be processed was sixteen (16) years of age. My folks did not have much money after paying off the bills, and I got tired of always wearing my cousin's Debra hand-me-downs year-after-year.

A project which is long gone called Henry Horner in Chicago, Illinois had a social center that contains a library. I was hired as a librarian's assistant and was responsible for re-shelving books and serving as a messenger. Libraries and social centers are considered NFPs. I had no idea that the pathway laid out to me would be where I would spend majority of my work experience. After that, I attended Lucy Flower High School another NFP organization.

Some schools are NFPs. It was in my sophomore year that my biology teacher Patricia Barto approached me about signing up into a work study program in which she trained young girls in laboratory procedures. The study programed allowed me to receive laboratory instructions in my junior year of high school. In my senior year, I was assigned to a hospital to receive additional training as a paid position. When it came time to graduate, I had a high school diploma with a trade cooperative laboratory program, and had obtained both the education and experience to be employable as a laboratory assistant. It would be up to the hospital to continue to employ me if they so desired.

The hospital in which I received training was Mary Thompson Hospital located on the west side of Chicago. However, prior to my senior year, during the summer, Ms. Barto would send me to the University of Illinois for a summer job to train in the Microbiology Department. In the fall of my senior year, I was sent to Thompson. I remained there two more additional years after my high school graduation, and the pathologist talked me into going to college to obtain a degree and to become a medical laboratory technician. I studied for the state board certification to receive the stamp of approval by the American Society of Clinical Pathologists also known as ASCP which you carried behind your name that you are both certified and registered.

Hospitals are also NFPs. A tender trap was laid for me. Years later, I would work at Mount Sinai Hospital, Cook County Hospital, and my last hospital stint was Rush-Presbyterian St. Luke, which has now been renamed Rush Medical Center. I would serve a total of twelve (12) years in the healthcare industry. A door supernaturally opened for me to replace my teacher Ms. Patricia Barto, and I returned to the other side of the desk as both a science teacher and the coordinator of the various programs in which I was a student. I would be the first ever hired Medical Laboratory Technician, ASCP with the Chicago Public School System which is another NFP venture. I served there for nine years, and later became employed at Morton Career Academy as a school guidance counselor and health career teacher – another NFP. I served a total of twelve (12) years with the CPS system in Chicago. Afterwards, I accepted my calling to ministry, and I became an ordained minister at a church on the west side of Chicago – another NFP stint.

The church housed and operated a community social center agency that had a youth program, food distribution, mentoring program, counseling, and other activities. I held a position as the program director – another NFP stint. I would serve a total of nineteen (19) years at that ministry and moved forward to serve at other churches and social service agencies. Later, I had the opportunity to serve as a chaplain at jails and prisons. Yes, another NFP setting.

So, you see, there are different types of NFPs. We are surrounded by them and the NFPs greatly impact our lives daily. Several years later, I started up two NFPs, and later became a NFP consultant and assist people to open NFPs by incorporating and obtaining their 501(c)(3) tax-exempt determination.

What do all these places have in common? They all serve and help people. There is no self-gain or profiting. In each instance, I received a salary, but nothing to make me a millionaire as one would have the opportunity of being if they hang their shingles in the For-Profit business. So, there you have it. Unknowingly, I had worked and served in NFP for over thirty (30) years of my life. Now, I am helping others to serve as well. I am known also as a For Profit also known as FP business. I am now on the other side of the corporation arena.

I wrote this book because when I ventured out to start up my first NFP, I could not find detailed information in the setup process. I would find a piece of information here or a piece of information there. I found out a lot of things on the administrative side of NFP by trial and error. After becoming a consultant, many clients trying to obtain funding, embarked on bits and pieces as well. Each ended up with fines or missing major elements in their set ups. There were a lot of doubling back, and cementing cracks in their foundations because each one lacked the knowledge that was needed.

I visited a lot of bookstores and there would be a few books on the shelves and the books were outdated. So, I decided to put together a step-by-step instruction manual in putting a NFP together to help people tie-up loose ends. However, laws and regulations are constantly changing, so it's very important that service providers, especially administrative staff, stay abreast of new policies by periodically checking websites of the Secretary of State, Attorney General's Office, and service to the Internal Revenue. In addition, it's important to have a membership with NFP associations, and to attend seminars sharing the latest that has come out of the Capitol in Washington. One must stay up-to-date about what is new on the Horizon especially when we elect new presidents.

Whenever, we have new presidents, there is also a new administration, new cabinet members, etc., therefore, resulting in new policies and regulations in all industries especially the NFPs. The presiding pages will give you insights and food-for-thought regarding NFP. You may decide after reading this book that a NFP is not for you. That is okay. It's best to know than to invest hundreds and often thousands of dollars into a NFP venture. Whatever the case, you may now begin your journey.

I have been intrigued by NFP. The NFP career route is for those that want to make a difference in SOMEONE's WORLD, whether a single mom, a lonely senior, a troubled youth, and an ex-offender seeking to re-enter society looking for a second chance. If you are a people person this is the career path for you. If you do not like working with the public, PLEASE, PRETTY PLEASE, keep walking because you will do more harm than good. After reading this book, please ponder, and do a self-evaluation as to whether this would be for you.

What are the pitfalls? Long hours, low wages, sacrifices, sleepless nights, overload of cases, and shoe-string budgets. You must be inventive, creative, resourceful, and an innovator. In addition, you need to be tenacious, resilient, persistent, and a warrior. You cannot be a whiner. You must see the glass half full. You must fight to the death. Some things you will not and have not learned in college.

You may have degrees, experiences, good communication written and oral, including soft skills. All those are great skills to have but are still not enough. You must be willing to run through troops and leap over walls. You must be that energized bunny that we all have seen on commercials. You cannot be a quitter. You must stay focused to succeed if not you will be crushed so do the world and all of us a favor, examine yourself as to whether the NFP arena is for you. Examine your motives and your intent as well.

What are the benefits? You get to see lives change. The NFP can be fulfilling. I saw very sick patients go home healed and happy. As a teacher, I encountered a youth that wanted to kill another student. After our time together discussing the issue, she changed her mind. I helped a foster child get her senior yearbook because her mom did not have any money. I also held a student in my arms whose mom had not been home for days because she walked the street at night. She was able to smile and finish her assignments and graduate. I saw over one thousand clients per month who received food from the food pantry that I operated. Those clients thanked me and the organization for being there for them because they had to decide whether to pay their rent or eat. I saw many men, women, boys, and girls give their lives to Christ. I saw single parents lift their heads in hope for a brighter future not just for their children but for them as well. I shed tears of joy when students walked across the stage and received their high school diplomas and went on to college and received their degrees.

The NFP route can be fulfilling other than draining at times. In looking back, I would not have had it any other way. While reading this material, make your decision. I applaud you for picking up a copy of this book.

**Write some ideas that would benefit the public and how you can help.**

## I. THE ORIGIN OF NOT-FOR-PROFIT

Whether one wants to admit it or not, the NFP origin is associated with the Jewish people after the great exodus. Once Jews entered CANAAN, the promise land, each tribe had their own parcel of land, and each family unit had their own strip of land that had been planted and due a bountiful harvest. The children of Israel were a group of agricultural people. God had commanded them to remember the poor and allow them to glean off the land. And whenever a brother or sister was sold into slavery at an appointed time, they were supposed to be released from their debt and have charity extended toward them. You can read more about the charitable acts that were a requirement to perform in one of the books of Moses entitled Leviticus where laws were given to them by God. We follow many of the Levitical laws today. You can read about sanitary laws, dietary laws, civil laws, moral laws, spiritual laws, etc.

If we fast forward passed biblical times we will discover that charitable, educational, and religious NFPs are thousands of years old, and the largest is the Catholic Church. Within the United States of America, NFP establishments date back as far as colonial times. Amongst the first is Harvard University. In fact, over ninety percent (90%) of the NFPs also known as non-governmental organizations have been established since 1950; however, NFP did not become regulated and unified until the early 1970.

In addition, numerous churches in England conducted charitable activities. Each church formed a group of people who did not want to be ministers or church workers that wanted to do charitable activities outside of the confinement of the walls of the church. In other words, they wanted the opportunity to provide services without having to be a church. The scope is wide from small grass roots with no assets, to NFP with multimillion dollar structures, universities, and religious orders. The NFP supports a range from private contributions, sales from goods and some services, grants, and governmental agencies.

The term NFP also covers sorority, fraternity, masons, associations, cemeteries, civic groups, scientific research groups, hospitals, symphonies, and even alcoholic anonymous. Any group that has a charitable aspect can be deemed a NFP and is eligible to apply for the 501(c)(3) tax-exempt status which is so coveted.

**What did you get from The Origin of NFP:** _______________________________

_______________________________________________________________

_______________________________________________________________

_______________________________________________________________

_______________________________________________________________

_______________________________________________________________

_______________________________________________________________

_______________________________________________________________

## II. TYPES OF NOT-FOR-PROFIT

Since NFP has been around for centuries throughout the world, there are many different types of NFPs and some would surprise you. The most common are churches, ministries, hospitals, social service agencies, and most schools. There are lodges, civil centers, the arts, cultural centers, multimedia centers, research organizations, and others. You may wonder how a hospital is a NFP, yet people are billed? Well, when you are serving a community and you do not turn anyone away, services are being rendered to those who can pay and to those who cannot pay. Hospitals are also known to provide free health educational workshops, free health fairs, free screenings usually diabetes, blood pressure, mammogram, and other services to the community. A NFP must include some free services.

Annually, hospitals review records and forgive a percentage of large debts; therefore, they can be listed as a NFP. However, not all NFPs are tax-exempt. You must qualify and read the "IRS Publication 557" for eligibility requirement. What is certain is that you must be incorporated prior to filing Form 1023 which is also known as the 501(c)(3) application. Should you apply, it is not guaranteed. It is imperative to meet the standards for the 501(c)(3) determination. If you plan to still run your NFP, although, you do not meet the standards for the 501(c)(3), it is a requirement to incorporate regardless.

It is imperative to become incorporated with the state in which you intend for the NFP to operate and provide services. If you operate and are caught, you will be shut down, receive a fine and penalty, and be barred in some instances of ever operating a NFP. Now that you are aware of the legalities, you need to decide what services you intend to provide and to what target group, along with the specific location.

Think of a name you want for the organization. Once you select a name for the NFP, a name check must be conducted with the secretary of state. If the name is used by another organization, it is not available to you. However, you do not have to lose heart. If it's a name you really like, you can either add another name, or number to it which would distinguish it from that NFP. You must type or write in black ink the selected name for the NFP that you and the board have chosen.

**What form do you have to fill-out to apply for a 501(c)(3) status?**

_________________________________________________________________

_________________________________________________________________

**Write several business names that would be a good name for your NFP:**

_________________________________________________________________

_________________________________________________________________

_________________________________________________________________

_________________________________________________________________

_________________________________________________________________

_________________________________________________________________

## III. NAME

You may choose any name if it is distinguishable from the name of an existing corporation, a foreign corporation authorized to conduct business affairs in the state in which the NFP will provide services. No name shall contain the words Democrat, regular democrat, democratic, republican or the name of any other established political party unless consent is given by the State Central Committee of such established party. The name that is chosen for a NFP must end with the letters NFP if the corporate name contains any word or phrase that indicates or implies that the corporation is organized for any purpose other than a purpose for which corporations may be organized under the Business Corporation Act. You may find out the availability of a name by writing or calling the Secretary of State's office in your state. A preliminary check also may be done on the Secretary of State's website in the state the NFP will be ran.

You may include a brief written request, listing the name and a brief description of the corporate purpose. You may reserve a name, if available for a period of ninety (90) days for a fee. You must submit a written request that list the name and a brief description of the NFP purpose. In other words, explain why the NFP was formed. There are no limitations to the number of times you can reserve a name.

## IV. BOARD

The NFP does not belong to you or the board members. All NFPs belong to the people of that state for which the NFP resides. Every NFP must have a board, and it is suggested that the initial board consists of three members. It is in the first meeting that you discuss the name, vision, mission, program activities, and the target population that you will provide services. You are not limited to having three board members; however, your board members should be in odd numbers.

Although board members can live in other states and even countries; however, one must be a resident in which the NFP resides. Your board members can be professionals such as doctors, lawyers, CPAs, etc., and can include community members, activists, and others. Your board can be one race or multicultural. It is suggested that you have a mixture of professionals and nonprofessionals, male & female, multicultural, and different socio-economic backgrounds. Whatever the case, you will need a working board.

The board should be a group of people that bring talents, knowledge, skills, abilities, and DEFINITELY MONEY also known as FUNDINGS, and essential contacts into the organization. You do not want dead weight on your board of directors. The governmental entities such as the Secretary of State, IRS, and others only recognize the position of President, Secretary, Treasurer, and Directors of the organization. Any other titles are known as in-house. In addition, you should give each person a description of their anticipated position, and a set of Bylaws which also describe their duties and the laws that govern your organization.

**Should the number of your board members be an even or odd number:**

_______________________________________________________________

**The laws that govern your NFP are called:** _______________________________

_______________________________________________________________

_______________________________________________________________

## V. MINUTES

Prior to incorporating, you should take minutes that show your intent of formation of a NFP. The minutes should go as following:

- Date of meeting;
- Location of meeting place;
- Time of meeting;
- Open meeting with Robert Rules for parliamentary meetings;
- Those present;
- Intent of meeting;
- List of what was covered;
- Notation of being an initial meeting;
- Selection of officers;
- Selection of a registered agent;
- Selection of location of the NFP;
- NFP Vision Statement;
- NFP Mission Statement;

- Program narratives (organization intended target population and activities);
- Resolution to any conflicts that occurred in the meeting;
- Forwarding of topics for next meeting;
- Next tentative meeting date;
- Name and title of person that took notes; and
- End of meeting.

### INTENT OF FORMATION OF A NFP
### MEETING MINUTES

**DATE OF MEETING** ______ / ______ / _________________

**LOCATION OF MEETING PLACE** _______________________________________________
_____________________________________________________________

**TIME OF MEETING** _______________________________________________

**OPEN MEETING WITH ROBERT RULES FOR PARLIAMENTARY**
_______________________________________________
_______________________________________________
_______________________________________________
_______________________________________________
_______________________________________________

**THOSE PRESENT**

NAME:_________________________________ TITLE ________________

NAME:_________________________________ TITLE ________________

NAME:_________________________________ TITLE ________________

NAME:_________________________________ TITLE ________________

NAME:_________________________________ TITLE ________________

NAME:_________________________________ TITLE ________________

NAME:_________________________________ TITLE ________________

NAME:_________________________________ TITLE ________________

# RESOURCE DEVELOPMENT
## GOING TO THE NEXT LEVEL

NAME:_________________________________ TITLE _______________

NAME:_________________________________ TITLE _______________

NAME:_________________________________ TITLE _______________

NAME:_________________________________ TITLE _______________

NAME:_________________________________ TITLE _______________

NAME:_________________________________ TITLE _______________

**INTENT OF MEETING**
_______________________________________________________
_______________________________________________________
_______________________________________________________
_______________________________________________________

**LIST OF WHAT WAS COVERED**

1.____________________________________________________
2.____________________________________________________
3.____________________________________________________
4.____________________________________________________
5.____________________________________________________
6.____________________________________________________
7.____________________________________________________
8.____________________________________________________

**NOTATION OF BEING AN INITIAL MEETING**
_______________________________________________________
_______________________________________________________

**SELECTION OF OFFICERS**

NAME:_________________________________ TITLE _______________

NAME:_________________________________ TITLE _______________

NAME:_________________________________ TITLE _______________

NAME:_________________________________ TITLE _______________

NAME:_________________________________ TITLE _______________

# RESOURCE DEVELOPMENT
## GOING TO THE NEXT LEVEL

NAME:_______________________________ TITLE _______________

NAME:_______________________________ TITLE _______________

NAME:_______________________________ TITLE _______________

NAME:_______________________________ TITLE _______________

NAME:_______________________________ TITLE _______________

NAME:_______________________________ TITLE _______________

NAME:_______________________________ TITLE _______________

NAME:_______________________________ TITLE _______________

**SELECTION OF A REGISTERED AGENT**
_____________________________________________________

**SELECTION OF LOCATION OF THE NFP**
_____________________________________________________
_____________________________________________________
_____________________________________________________

**NFP VISION STATEMENT**
_____________________________________________________
_____________________________________________________
_____________________________________________________
_____________________________________________________
_____________________________________________________
_____________________________________________________
_____________________________________________________

**NFP MISSION STATEMENT**
_____________________________________________________
_____________________________________________________
_____________________________________________________
_____________________________________________________
_____________________________________________________
_____________________________________________________

**PROGRAM NARRATIVES (ORGANIZATION**
POPULATION_________________________________________
_____________________________________________________

**INTENDED TARGET POPULATION AND ACTIVITIES)**

_______________________________________________
_______________________________________________
_______________________________________________
_______________________________________________

ACTIVITIES_______________________________________
_______________________________________________
_______________________________________________
_______________________________________________
_______________________________________________
_______________________________________________
_______________________________________________

**RESOLUTION TO ANY CONFLICTS THAT OCCURRED IN THE MEETING**

_______________________________________________
_______________________________________________
_______________________________________________
_______________________________________________
_______________________________________________
_______________________________________________
_______________________________________________
_______________________________________________
_______________________________________________
_______________________________________________
_______________________________________________
_______________________________________________

**FORWARDING OF TOPICS FOR NEXT MEETING**

_______________________________________________
_______________________________________________
_______________________________________________
_______________________________________________
_______________________________________________
_______________________________________________
_______________________________________________
_______________________________________________

**NEXT TENTATIVE MEETING DATE**   _______/_______/_______________

**NAME AND TITLE OF PERSON THAT TOOK NOTES END OF MEETING**

NAME:_________________________________ TITLE _______________

_______________________________________________

_______________________________________
_______________________________________
_______________________________________
_______________________________________
_______________________________________
_______________________________________

It is during this initial board meeting that those who are present and selected to serve as officials and directors, can sign the incorporation papers. Information regarding the incorporation papers will be covered later.

The organization secretary is responsible for typing, and filing away the minutes of the organization, which is now a legal document that can be subpoenaed by the court system. One month before the next board meeting, letters are to be mailed to board members along with previous minutes, and an agenda which list items to be discussed and covered in the upcoming meetings.

**List names of officials and directors of the NFP:**

_______________________________________

_______________________________________

_______________________________________

_______________________________________

_______________________________________

_______________________________________

_______________________________________

## VI. VISION STATEMENT

Every NFP should have a vision statement. It is generally futuristic and describes where the organization would like to be in five (5), ten (10), and twenty (20) years. A vision statement provides the future state of an organization. Below is an example of a Vision Statement:

**FRESH START NFP Vision Statement:**

> The FRESH START NFP will have national offices throughout the United States of America which will offer agglomerate of program services to provide recovery treatment programs which will result in a fresh start in life.

**Write your NFP Vision Statement:**

_______________________________________________

_______________________________________________

_______________________________________________

_______________________________________________

_______________________________________________

**Write your NFP Vision Statement in 5 years, 10 years, and 20 years:**

5 Years: _______________________________________

_______________________________________________

_______________________________________________

10 Years: ______________________________________

_______________________________________________

_______________________________________________

_______________________________________________

20 Years: ______________________________________

_______________________________________________

_______________________________________________

_______________________________________________

_______________________________________________

## VII.   MISSION STATEMENT

Every nonprofit organization must have a mission statement. It is generally one or two sentences that clearly state the organization's purpose. A mission statement provides the present state of an organization. Below is an example of a mission statement:

**FRESH START NFP Mission Statement:**

All people have the right to be self-sufficient with self-esteem. Still today, many people suffering from alcohol and drug abuse are lacking a sense of self-worth, because they cannot pay for adequate treatment for recovery.

FRESH START offers these people an opportunity for recovery and positive changes through affordable, effective counseling and therapy to restore an individual's sense of responsibility and self-worth.

**Write your Mission Statement Purpose:**

_______________________________________________

_______________________________________________

_______________________________________________

_______________________________________________

_______________________________________________

## VIII.   SECRETARY OF STATE

Every state within the United States has a state agency known as the Secretary of State. Whatever state you intend to incorporate the NFP organization, should be done through that secretary of state's office. You just simply ask for an application to form a NFP.

If you are not incorporated and decide to operate as a NFP and it is found out by the state, you can be shut down and be given a hefty fine. The NFP must be recognized on the state level first by the Secretary of State.

## IX. ARTICLES OF INCORPORATION

The document that is used to incorporate the NFP is known as the Articles of Incorporation, now there are other documents of formations. However, the most common formation is the articles of incorporation and that will be discussed later in the book. Articles of Incorporation is usually a one sheet document front and back and is relatively easy to fill out. We will explore each section. To file this document with the Secretary of State, a filing fee is charged.

### A.      Corporation Name and Address

There are two types of corporations in the United States: foreign and domestic. Foreign corporations are those that operate outside of the United States, although, their paperwork has been completed within the states. There are domestic corporations which are those NFPs that are located and operate within the United States.

Under the term domestic corporations, you have what is known as For-Profit (order my book titled "For-Profit Business" for more information) and NFP also known as Nonprofit. We are covering in this book NFP formation and other pertinent information to assist you in your startup venture. When the focus is on NFP, there were a variety that were covered earlier such as churches, some schools, hospitals, cultural centers, art institutes, museums, lodges, etc.

Before filing the Articles of Incorporation, it is best to do a name check. I would like to share a situation where a name check was not conducted, and an organization ended up in court, heavily fined, and ordered to not use the name. An overzealous community member with limited NFP experience did not do a name check. Well, five years down the line that individual had left the position and the organization received a letter from the Secretary of State to inform the organization that the name was already in use. The organization received a fine.

Here is another incident: There was a social service agency with the same identical name as someone who had the name first and had been operating for over twenty-five (25) years. The executive director of that organization contacted the agency and requested that they change the name. Well, they refused to do so and were dragged into court. The judge ruled in favor of the older NFP and fined the organization. The court also told the other NFP to cease operating in that name. The organization regrouped, kept the name and added some distinguishing factors to it. Remember if a name is being used and you like it, you can keep it by adding to it; which is legal.

**List Several Names that Describe Your NFP:**

__________________________________________________________

__________________________________________________________

__________________________________________________________

__________________________________________________________

Next list the principal office location of the NFP. It can be an administrative office where there are no programs onsite or programs can be taking place onsite. Some NFPs have several locations; although, you must provide the main location on the application.

**Address of the Main Location is:**

__________________________________________________________

__________________________________________________________

__________________________________________________________

__________________________________________________________

**List Other Locations Here, if any:**

__________________________________________________________

______________________________________________

______________________________________________

______________________________________________

______________________________________________

## B.    Registered Agent

The purpose of requiring each corporation to maintain a registered agent and a registered location is for public record where service of process against the corporation and such person may be found. This person also is the one to whom official correspondence may be found. Also, this person is the one to whom official correspondence from the Secretary of State is sent. However, there are qualifications that must be met to be a registered agent.

## C.    Registered Agent's Address Qualifications

A registered agent must be a residence of the state for which the NFP will reside and provide services. The registered agent must be at least eighteen (18) years of age. The registered agent can also be a listed corporation.

The registered office of the agent must be within the state of which the NFP resides and a street or road address is to be provided, A Post Office box number is not acceptable. After listing the corporate name and address, a registered agent must be listed. This is no more than a contact person. This is a person who receives the organization's mail, and serves as a contact. You can either use the registered agent personal address or the address of the NFP location. If changes need to be made regarding either, the registered agent or the office, the change must be reported as soon as possible. Prompt reporting of changes is important to ensure that correspondence will not be delayed or lost.

You must select the intended duration of the NFP. The duration is the period you plan to be incorporated. The duration is perpetual, unless otherwise stated in the Articles of Incorporation. The term perpetual means ongoing and endless.

## D.    Initial Board Members

The board members' printed names, signatures, addresses, cities, states, and zip codes must appear on the incorporation papers. Caution: if you are setting up and spearheading your organization, and this is your vision, you must be included on the board. It is suggested that you be the registered agent as well; or you can assign that task to another and appear on the board only. However, if you appear as the registered agent only and not on the board, you have no voice and you will not be able to offer any suggestions and ideas.

## E.    Project Activities

You must state that your organization is charitable or a private foundation, describe your target population, and the services to be rendered. The target population described can be children and youths, homeless, victims of domestic violence, seniors, women, men, gang members, etc. Describe the services to be rendered such as shelter also known as dormitory, supportive services, case managements, arts, housings, after school programs, transportations, daycare, etc. The sharing of this information should be found in both your vision and mission statements. You are revealing the purpose for which the NFP is formed.

## F.    SIGNATURES

It is important that you have the signatures, addresses, cities, states, and zip codes of the board members on the incorporation document. The paperwork should be filled out in duplicates. If you do not have their signatures, the application will not be filed. Once you are processed, the state will keep a copy and stamp the other forms and send to you with an announcement letter that you are now incorporated in the state for which the NFP resides.

## X. CERTIFICATE OF GOOD STANDING

This is a needful document especially when it is time for you to seek funding. A Certificate of Good Standing is a document that will let the funder know that the NFP for which the state resides is still incorporated and not dissolved. Contact the secretary of state in your area to obtain the certificate of good standing. A small fee is required.

## XI. IN CONCLUSION OF NFP INCORPORATION

The information given above describes the information which all states have in their incorporation papers. The formats may be slightly different, but each form contains the same requirements that are stated above. In addition, there may be a question asking if you are a type of an association, in which you should answer accordingly. In most cases, the answer will be "No."

Due to everyone being cost-conscious, states are streamlining and have created one form where you can check off NFP or FP then proceed to answer the applicable questions that pertains to the NFP.

Becoming a NFP organization is like a two-sided coin. It will benefit the public and, also be rewarding seeing others change for the betterment of mankind. The team effort of the Board Members will help make the NFP organization effective.

From time to time, review the Vision Statement and Mission Statement to be sure you are focused on the reason the NFP was formed.

If you chose not to obtain a 501(c)(3), taxes will be due. In the following section, I will discuss further how to obtain a 501(c)(3).

# NFP 501(c)(3)

## I.  WHY A 501(C)(3)

Why a 501(c)(3)? Is it necessary to apply for the 501(c)(3) from the internal revenue service when you are applying for a NFP? No. Once you are incorporated by the state in which your NFP resides, you can legally operate within your state as a NFP. However, if anyone gives you donations, it is not tax deductible. In other words, there are no write-offs for the individual also known as private contributors, businesses, foundations, or Funders. Therefore, it is somewhat of a *catch-22* (a dilemma where there is no escape) situation. It has also been cited that churches are not required to have it either once again, it's a *catch-22*.

## II.  IRS

The IRS have several departments and it is very important that you contact and have your paperwork sent to the correct division, and that you speak with the correct IRS agent. I have heard so many horror stories. We will look at one case before concluding the information that will be shared. The IRS has two (2) main divisions when it comes to tax reporting. The FOR PROFIT and the NOT-FOR-PROFIT. The reporting of both is different. When you have a 501(c)(3), you are tax-exempt. The IRS wants you to file information of donations that comes into your organization so keep a record of the sponsors and the amounts of each donation. Those records of donations are called gross receipts.

**Donors' Name:** _________________________________________________________
**Donation Amount:** ___________________________________________________
**Address:** ___________________________________________________
**Email Address:** ___________________________________________________
**Phone No.:** ___________________________________________________

**Donors' Name:** ___________________________________________________
**Donation Amount:** ___________________________________________________
**Address:** ___________________________________________________
**Email Address:** ___________________________________________________
**Phone No.:** ___________________________________________________

**Donors' Name:** ___________________________________________________
**Donation Amount:** ___________________________________________________
**Address:** ___________________________________________________
**Email Address:** ___________________________________________________
**Phone No.:** ___________________________________________________

**Donors' Name:** ___________________________________________________
**Donation Amount:** ___________________________________________________
**Address:** ___________________________________________________
**Email Address:** ___________________________________________________
**Phone No.:** ___________________________________________________

**Donors' Name:** ______________________________
**Donation Amount:** ______________________________
**Address:** ______________________________
**Email Address:** ______________________________
**Phone No.:** ______________________________

**Donors' Name:** ______________________________
**Donation Amount:** ______________________________
**Address:** ______________________________
**Email Address:** ______________________________
**Phone No.:** ______________________________

**Donors' Name:** ______________________________
**Donation Amount:** ______________________________
**Address:** ______________________________
**Email Address:** ______________________________
**Phone No.:** ______________________________

**Donors' Name:** ______________________________
**Donation Amount:** ______________________________
**Address:** ______________________________
**Email Address:** ______________________________
**Phone No.:** ______________________________

Churches are exempt from filing what is known as an annual report. All other charities as well as public and private foundations are required to submit an annual report. The filing of the annual report is completed on a 990, 990 EZ, or 990-N Electronic Filing. The 990 is a full form to record monetary and properties donations. The 990 EZ is a short form that is usually one page. You file either of these when donations are being $50,000 or more. There is the 990-N Electronic Filing, which is an electronic form to be completed online and filled out when the organization has received funding under $50,000. If you miss three (3) consecutive years of filing, the 501(c)(3) is revoked.

It will also be helpful to subscribe to the IRS newsletter and periodically check www.IRS.gov to read continual updates. IRS is constantly making changes in their policies and as stated in an earlier section; whenever we elect a new president, policies change as well as a new administration. The lack of knowledge of the most current best practices will not cut it. If you do not keep up-to-date and a violation happens, there may be hefty penalties. When you log on to the government's website, you can search for CHARITIES and NON-FOR-PROFITS to review updates.

As mentioned before, FOR PROFIT. The FOR PROFITs are required to complete tax reporting of the earnings of their business(es), and pay their taxes according to their business structure. In my book titled, "For Profit," I will cover more information regarding tax reporting of earnings.

## III. BENEFITS OF 501(c)(3)

Now, I will share a case study about Pastor Yakes and the XYZ Church of God & Christ. A new member who is an accountant, which was excited, approached the pastor of the church asking if the church had been paying any taxes. The pastor allows the member to review all church fiscal records. After reviewing the records, the accountant concludes and prepares a tax report on behalf of the church for the pastor. Several months later, the pastor is contacted by the IRS and is informed that a substantial amount of taxes is owed.

I was in a restaurant when the pastor approached me remembering the type of work that I do, and we set up an appointment. He confides in me the dilemma. After reviewing all records that he has a 501(c)(3), I reminded him therefore, the contributions are tax-exempt, and all he must do is inform the IRS and give the For-Profit Tax Division a copy of his 501(c)(3) determination letter and the nightmare would go away. He goes back to the member who is an accountant and the accountant chose to do something else. Three (3) days later, the IRS is on his doorstep to confiscate the church, rental properties, his home, and van.

A most common problem that I have found is that people consult lawyers, CPAs, and accountants that do not have a NFP background. If you are going to use the services of any of these professionals, make sure someone is knowledgeable and experienced in the NFP arena. The accountant submitted documentation to the IRS as if the church was a FOR PROFIT business instead of presenting the church as a NOT-FOR-PROFIT with a 501(c)(3).

**Why is the 501(c)(3) important?** ________________________________

________________________________________________________

________________________________________________________

## IV. EMPLOYER IDENTIFICATION NUMBER (EIN)

After becoming incorporated through your state, you need to move forward and obtain an EIN which stands for Employer Identification Number. Just think of it as a business social security number. An EIN is assigned to your NFP so that it will be identifiable and distinguished from other organizations. The EIN is very important for without it your 501(c)(3) application will not be processed. If you ever must contact the IRS to discuss your organization, the first thing the IRS agent asks before pulling up your file is, the EIN.

This number is also important in tax reporting season. Although you are a 501(c)(3) tax-exempt organization, you are still required to submit a report to the IRS. This informs the IRS of the amount of gross receipts that your organization attained. Thus, you are reporting the amount of donations that came into the organization.

If your organization is a 501(c)(3) and it receives below $50,000, you would file taxes electronically using the 990E-Postcard. If your organization received over $50,000, you must submit either the 990 or 990 EZ by mail. This is subject to change because most companies are doing everything online.

Please note, if the tax year <u>ends in December,</u> the deadline for completing and submitting any of the 990s **is May 15th**. If the tax year <u>ends in July,</u> the deadline for completing and submitting any of the 990s is **by December 15th**. Five months after your fiscal year ends and on the 15th day.

If you do not attain the 501(c)(3) tax-exempt status any donations over $650 that comes into the organization, taxes are required to be paid both to the state and to the federal government.

The benefit of the 501(c)(3) determination tax-exempt services is that an organization is exempt from paying both state and federal taxes of funding. Hence, when an organization does not have the 501(c)(3) exemption status, whatever funding comes into the organization, state and federal taxes must get paid on those funds.

Another benefit of having the 501(c)(3) status is that your organization will be eligible for sales tax exemption; which means that when you purchase items from a vendor, stores, etc., you will not be required to pay taxes just pay for the purchases.

The purchases must be on behalf of the organization and for organizational purposes only. For example, if you have a youth after school program, the items purchased should reflect the services that are being offered to the youth. Items cannot be purchased for the use of staff, volunteers, or board members but for the target population for which services are intended. The items that can be bought for the organization can range from office equipment, office supplies, household products, personal hygiene products, vehicles, real estates, etc.

The 501(c)(3) is also helpful in assisting organizations that own real estates to be exempt from paying property taxes, and water bills. You must check within your state and see all that is offered to 501(c)(3) NFP. The 501(c)(3) can be used to obtain free or reduce leasing opportunities such as office space and rental for gala events.

The 501(c)(3) organizations are also eligible to use meeting rooms of public libraries for free. The park district, offers reduce rates for rentals of events. The United States Postal Service offers reduce bulk mail rate to 501(c)(3) NFP.

**1.** What comes first the 501(c)(3) or the EIN?

_______________________________________________________

**2.** When are you able to file your gross receipts (taxes) online?

_______________________________________________________

_______________________________________________________

_______________________________________________________

---

**3.** What is one of the benefits of having a tax-exempt status?

---


---

## V. 501(C)(3) APPLICATION

The 501(c)(3) application is also known as Form 1023. It looks like a booklet and comes with an instruction section. The instruction section is the beginning pages, and there is the actual application that has nine sections that consist of twelve (12) pages. It usually takes over forty (40) hours to complete the pages.

Page one (1) consist of the organization's general information, Page two (2) is where you would answer questions as to whether you are a corporation and if so which type, if you have bylaws, including questions about clauses, there is a section to list the board members, their positions, addresses, and if the board members are to receive compensations. Page three (3) has questions about the highest paid employee or contractor to receive salary. Next is a series of conflict of interest, policies, and other questions are asked from page four (4) to page eight (8). On page eight (8) there are questions about the organization's assets if you have any and whether you are a public charity or a private foundation. On page nine (9) you will find a projected budget which will reflect your activities, how will your organization receive and support your programs, and the remaining pages require an authorized officer's position and signature.

In addition, there is a checklist to ensure that you have everything in the envelope which you plan to mail off to the IRS. The checklist ranges from organization information, EIN #, power of attorney, schedules, etc. Just go to IRS.gov and do a search for Form 1023 and review the entire application. Once the application is completed, everything is placed inside a large envelope addressed to the IRS.

Now, the IRS charges what is called a user fee which is really a processing fee for them to review and release the 501(c)(3). Over one billion people apply for this document yearly; however, approximately

750,000 people are approved for the 501(c)(3) status. It is a tedious process and one must be familiar with the NFP language. NFPs are usually turned down for the following reasons:

1) Do not follow directions,
2) Do not answer all the questions,
3) Activities are not exempt activities,
4) Lack of NFP language,
5) Do not have a purpose clause,
6) Do not have a dissolution clause,
7) Do not enclose or forward bylaws,
8) Conflict of interest within the application,
9) Did not enclose the user fee, or
10) Did not enclose the appropriate user fee.

Unfortunately, some people do not know how to follow instructions which results in being denied. You are expected to answer ALL questions no matter if you feel that it was answered in another section of the application. Another reason for denial is that activities sound more like a for profit activity; therefore, making an organization sound like a business. In addition, it is wise to have someone with an educational background and experience or both, to complete the application.

Language! Language! Language! If you are not familiar with the NFP arena, you will not be able to accurately and satisfactorily answer the questions; same thing with proposal writing. The application and your Bylaws require a Purpose Clause. What is a purpose clause? It is the reason for which your organization was formed. The Purpose Clause is the activities that you describe with your Secretary of State.

A Dissolution Clause is also required within the 501(c)(3) application and the bylaws. You must have a dissolution clause that states that no one associated with the NFP whether an officer, board member, director, staff, or volunteers will not profit from the NFP. In the event, the NFP must dissolve, all monetary assets, in kind, equipment, supplies, properties, etc. must be given as donations to a NFP that has the similar mission of the defunct NFP. In other words, no one can decide to take computers, furniture, supplies, or items home after the NFP folds. There is no ownership in a NFP. The NFP belongs to the people within that state. Bylaws governs and set laws for the organization. It is also important to periodically update the organization's Bylaws.

In America on September 11 (911), congress passed a ruling that it must be included in all Bylaws that the NFP, for which you have been entrusted to oversee, will not do business nor allow networking or alliances with known terrorists. A statement of such must appear in the Bylaws along with a link that is provided. The link has a listing of a database of thousands of identified terrorists.

Recently, our government passed laws legalizing same sex marriage. If you are a church or ministry, you are required to put in your Bylaws that you will not conduct marriage ceremonies to people of the same sex along with biblical scriptures. Otherwise, you will have to do so, and it will be unlawful for you not to. I recommend that you periodically update your Bylaws especially when there is changing of the guards, hence a new administration.

Go to the IRS.gov website and monitor the public charities section. Register for the e-newsletter so you can stay up-to-date on information. I cannot stress enough the importance of staying informed.

In 2010 a lot of NFPs were caught off guard when a ruling was enacted that if a NFP missed three consecutive years of filing their 990s annual report, the 501(c)(3) will be revoked. In order to get reinstated, a new application will have to be submitted stating the reason why it was revoked and a plan explaining preventive measures to avoid being revoked again. In addition, a form for reinstatement must be completed, along with a fee of $400, $850, or whatever user fee is being charged based on your organization's budget. Please keep in mind, the user fee is subject to change, and I want to encourage you to retain the 501(c)(3) status.

There is a filing fee for the 501(c)(3) application. In 2004 the user fee was $150 for an organization's budget under $10,000, and $500 for an organization's budget of over $10,000. In the year 2016, if an organization's budget is under $10,000, the user fee was $400. If the budget is over $10,000, the user fee was $850. So, I hope that you see urgency in getting your NFP organization filed under a 501(c)(3).

Another reason that applicants are denied the tax-exempt status, the application shows conflict of interests. The IRS frowns on a board that consists of all family members. Family members can serve on the board but cannot make up the total board. The 501(c)(3) application will be declined

Another conflict of interest would be if the organization purchase and/or lease, goods, services, etc. from an officer, board member, director, staff, or volunteer. This is also a conflict of interest. In addition, there is a series of questions that can identify a conflict of interest. Believe it or not, terrorist activities are also a conflict of interest which can result in an investigation being launched against your NFP organization.

Another reason applications are denied the 501(c)(3) status, people forgot to include the user fee or the appropriate user fee, and/or the budget and program activities are not equivalent. The activities within the program services prices would be higher but being reported lower in describing the financials, therefore, resulting in a decline of the application.

Most of the time, an agent will send a letter about an issue that needs to be resolved about the application and usually gives thirty (30) days to resolve. If you need additional time, you can request an extension. The agent will also give you a window, usually a month, and if you successfully answered and addressed the issues at hand, the state will release the 501(c)(3) application within two (2) to four (4) weeks after the review.

Once an application is completed, there is a certain order in which the IRS requires each item to be placed inside the envelope. The following list is the requirement:

1) A letter size envelope which encloses the user fee in a cashier's check or money order (check irs.gov for the exact amount),
2) Check off list,
3) 501(c)(3) application also known as Form 1023,

4) Articles of Incorporation and amendments if applicable,
5) Bylaws,
6) Conflict of Interest Policy,
7) Program Narrative,
8) Fundraising Activity,
9) Any schedule if applicable (*e.g.*, churches and schools),
10) Additional information for churches, and
11) The signature of one board member preferably the president is required.


Not following the above order will result in a delay of your application in being reviewed and approved for the 501(c)(3) tax-exempt status.

The IRS does not want anything stapled, cut, or bound. In regards to the user fee, the IRS wants the fee to be placed in an envelope in front of the application. The check off list is for your benefit. If there are any amendments to the articles of incorporation, please include them. In addition, the IRS requires that when you are incorporating your NFP, a document is included which describes both the purpose and dissolution clauses that describes a dissolution clause and a statement that no one would profit from the NFP. The state is not going to tell you that. It is an IRS requirement. You must be aware and submit it along with the incorporation papers that you file. You must include a policy as to how conflict of interest is going to be avoided in the NFP and all associated with the NFP need to be aware of the policy and it should be enforced.

The program narrative consists of the activities or services in which you intend to provide, how often, what do that activity or service entails, who are the activities and services intended, and how many hours will be worked toward rendering of the services or activities. You may want to do a chart or diagram to make it easier for the IRS agent to visualize.

If you are a school, daycare, church, or housing service provider, additional information will be required, and you must determine which schedule within the 501(c)(3) application applies to you. Fill out the various questions that are pertinent to the mission, activities, and services of the NFP.

Unfortunately, people forget to sign the application for the 501(c)(3) tax-exempt determination. Therefore, the process cannot be completed although the application has a status of being satisfactorily reviewed. Usually when items are missing from the application it can result in a six (6) to eight (8) months delay before you are contacted by mail.

**List items that your NFP already owns:**

___________________________________________________________

___________________________________________________________

___________________________________________________________

___________________________________________________________

___________________________________________________________

___________________________________________________________

___________________________________________________________

**List items that you need to acquire in order to complete the previous list.**

___________________________________________________________

___________________________________________________________

___________________________________________________________

___________________________________________________________

___________________________________________________________

## VI. BYLAWS

The Internal Revenue Service requires three items to be in your Bylaws that are mandatory. Listed below are the items:

1) You must have a purpose clause. A purpose clause is simply giving the reason for which the organization was formed,

2) The target population to be served, the activities, programs, or program services to be rendered, and

3) The Dissolution clause.

If you do not have these items, you will be automatically declined for the 501(c)(3) determination tax-exempt status.

The first mandatory item is stating why your organization was formed. You are describing the type of organization that you are such as a church, social service, agency, school, cultural center, or other. You can describe what group of people the organization plans to serve which is known as the target population. The term is self-explanatory, in that you are describing the target population based on their socio-economic status, ethnicity, gender, or other factors which made you select that group of people to serve.

Do you want to serve seniors, children, youth, women, men, or those with low to moderate income? Do you want to serve the underprivileged, underserved, or the illiterate? You must list the services or programs that will be available for the target population. Are you going to provide educational services, housing, counseling, case management, reading program, GED, homework hotline, tutoring, or drama classes? Are you going to provide music composition, an afterschool program, shelter, transitional housing, or mentoring? You will need to describe those services which should be listed in your Articles of Incorporation on the state level, and now this will have to be described in the Bylaws of the organization, and the program narrative attachment of Form 1023, also known as, the 501(c)(3) application.

The second mandatory item is the purpose of the NFP. The purpose will state the activities. What are you going to do with the NFP? The activities can be a school program, mentoring, after school program, educational services, tutoring, community outreach, senior programs, housing services, food distribution, clothing closet, community garden, and the list goes on and on.

The third mandatory item is the Dissolution Clause. This Clause states that no one (which includes officers, board members, directors, staff, or volunteers) will profit, self-gain, or benefit from the NFP. If the NFP becomes dissolved, the assets of the organization will be transferred to a similar organization as stated earlier in the 501(c)(3) Application Section. What is a similar organization?

A similar organization is one that has the same mission as the organization that has become dissolved. The dissolved organization assets such as monetary, in-kind, properties, equipment, supplies, and any other items that belonged to the organization must be transferred to a similar organization. So, what does that means? There cannot be a board meeting where you all state, we are out of business and people get up from the table and start taking computers, equipment, supplies, and other items. Also, no one can purchase items in the name of the organization and take it home for other personal and/or business use. You can't buy a vehicle in the name of the organization and it's parked outside your door nightly, or going on a fishing trip with the vehicle. One must avoid personal gain as well as conflict of interest.

Included in the third item of the Bylaws, there must be a statement included that the NFP does not and will not support terrorist activities. There is a link that must appear in your Bylaws that leads to the database with thousands of known terrorists' names, along with their businesses that have been identified by homeland security. If you do not have these three mandatory items within the Bylaws, your application will be declined.

There are other items within the Bylaws such as protocol, officers, and their duties. The Bylaws usually covers how often the board meets. The IRS requires that all boards meet at least annually, I recommend that the board meet on a quarterly basis.

The Bylaws covers how to handle funds, resolve disputes, policies, regulations that discuss how the NFP should operate. The Bylaws should also describe how officers are selected, voted, and/or appointed and how long is the term of officers, etc. You must determine if the organization will have a membership.

A perfect example of a NFP with memberships, are churches. When it comes to operating a NFP with a membership, you must describe how members are selected and what are the requirements? (*E.g.*, members must do a registration and/or pay dues.) If you want to obtain information in the writing of Bylaws, google "sample of Bylaws for NFP" and a series of information will be available for you to examine and select what will work for the NFP which you have formed. Finally, it is important to update the Bylaws. It is recommended that the Bylaws are updated every three years.

Bylaws govern the organization. There have been situations where NFP's board members were at odds with each other and had to appear in court. The judge will always want to examine the Bylaws and if the situation is not addressed in the bylaws, the judge will make a ruling and it may not be favorable of the offended party. There have been cases where the board was wiped out and new people were appointed by the judge and the founder of the NFP was removed. Not a pretty sight. Therefore, it is important that every possible human issue that would surface should be addressed in the Bylaws. Otherwise, the court system will intercept.

## VII.    FUNDRAISING

The IRS will require a NFP to have a fundraising plan because they want to know how you intend to secure funds to operate and provide services. Below are several methods of fundraising. You may use some or all the ideas below, including other creative ideas:

**Mail Solicitation-** Once you have approval from the Secretary of State and the IRS, you can mail out letters to solicit donations through the United States Postal Office.

**Email-** You may send out solicitations to your email contacts providing that you avoid spam. Check with your service provider about sending out massive emails for the purposes of solicitation.

**Personal Solicitation-** You can seek the support of family members, neighbors, and other private contributors to your organization.

**Foundation Grants**- Once you have the tax-exemption status, you may seek a foundation grant maker who has the same mission statement as your organization. There are millions of foundations that seek to fund NFPs.

**Phone Solicitation**- You may solicit people by phone for contributions, but you must make sure that they are not on the national Do Not Call list. This may result in your organization being sued.

Organization Website- Your organization will be free to solicit donations through your website. You can put PayPal or other pay buttons and instructions for giving directly on your website.

Other Organizations Websites- It is permissible to receive donations from other websites. Hence, your web address can be placed on another company's website where you can receive contributions.

Governmental Grants- You can apply and submit grants to fund your organization's activities. You must register to be eligible to apply. You must obtain a Dun & Bradstreet number and SAM, and research the governmental department that fits your mission. (E.g., the Department of Health & Human Services, Department of Agriculture, and the Department of Public Health)

The president of the United States has a cabinet. The cabinet consists of twelve (12) people that are the head of twelve (12) governmental agencies and each agency provides grant money. Where does grant money come from? Grant money comes from taxes and from businesses that are looking for tax shelters. They promise to invest in the community in which their business resides and in doing so, tax breaks are given when they issue grants through foundations that are created by them. In addition, banks also issue grants to fund programs implemented by NFPs.

Other areas a NFP can receive funding are social media, Kickstarter, GoFundMe, Indiegogo, and other crowd funding investment angels that are social entrepreneurs. A lot of NFPs host galas, dinners, auctions, bake sales, Ad books, cake walks, candy sales and others. You can also use a kettle like the Salvation Army or have a coin machine at stores and cleaners to raise funds for your activities.

**Create two or three fundraising ideas that would help your NFP business:**

___________________________________________________________

___________________________________________________________

___________________________________________________________

___________________________________________________________

___________________________________________________________

___________________________________________________________

## VIII.  PROGRAM NARRATIVES

You are expected to provide a program narrative of past, present, or future services to be provided to the NFP's target population. You can do it in either a written narrative or graph format. Whatever the case, you need to list the activities, the staff/volunteers to carry out those activities, description of the activities, how often the activity will be conducted (weekly, bi-weekly, etc.), how much time will go into the activities (*e.g.*, eight (8) hours, thirty (30) minutes, etc.), and what percentage will that activity be in a forty (40) hour work week? Will it be ten percent (10%) of the work week or twenty-five percent (25%)? Next, state whether it is a tax-exempt activity and how will the service cost be handled (fee, grant money, public contributions, etc.). Lastly, who will oversee the program (*e.g.*, Executive Director, Program Director, or Supervisor)?

**Program Narrative of the Past is:** ___________________________________

___________________________________________________________

___________________________________________________________

**Program Narrative of the Present is:** _______________________________

___________________________________________________________

___________________________________________________________

**Program Narrative of the future is:** _______________________________

_______________________________________________________________

_______________________________________________________________

_______________________________________________________________

## IX. ANNUAL BUDGET

Form 1023, also known as, the 501(c)(3) application requires start up organizations to present a three (3) year projected budget. This consists of fiscal year beginning and fiscal year ending. There are columns in which items are listed. You would either respond with a numerical figure or zero. In this section of the 501(c)(3) application you can record potential contributions, fundraising costs, salaries, program services, etc., which you must give a dollar amount.

What constitutes a budget? Rent, leasing, telephones, utilities, insurance, salaries, equipment supplies, office furniture, program services, and more constitute a budget.

On the following page, you will find the first page of Form 1023 which requires your financial data of the NFP.

Form 1023 (Rev. 12-2013)   (00) Name: _______________________   EIN: _____ – _____   Page **9**

| Part IX | Financial Data |

For purposes of this schedule, years in existence refer to completed tax years. If in existence 4 or more years, complete the schedule for the most recent 4 tax years. If in existence more than 1 year but less than 4 years, complete the statements for each year in existence and provide projections of your likely revenues and expenses based on a reasonable and good faith estimate of your future finances for a total of 3 years of financial information. If in existence less than 1 year, provide projections of your likely revenues and expenses for the current year and the 2 following years, based on a reasonable and good faith estimate of your future finances for a total of 3 years of financial information. (See instructions.)

### A. Statement of Revenues and Expenses

| | Type of revenue or expense | Current tax year | 3 prior tax years or 2 succeeding tax years | | | | (e) Provide Total for (a) through (d) |
|---|---|---|---|---|---|---|---|
| | | (a) From ______ To ______ | (b) From ______ To ______ | (c) From ______ To ______ | (d) From ______ To ______ | | |
| **Revenues** | | | | | | | |
| 1 | Gifts, grants, and contributions received (do not include unusual grants) | | | | | | |
| 2 | Membership fees received | | | | | | |
| 3 | Gross investment income | | | | | | |
| 4 | Net unrelated business income | | | | | | |
| 5 | Taxes levied for your benefit | | | | | | |
| 6 | Value of services or facilities furnished by a governmental unit without charge (not including the value of services generally furnished to the public without charge) | | | | | | |
| 7 | Any revenue not otherwise listed above or in lines 9–12 below (attach an itemized list) | | | | | | |
| 8 | Total of lines 1 through 7 | | | | | | |
| 9 | Gross receipts from admissions, merchandise sold or services performed, or furnishing of facilities in any activity that is related to your exempt purposes (attach itemized list) | | | | | | |
| 10 | Total of lines 8 and 9 | | | | | | |
| 11 | Net gain or loss on sale of capital assets (attach schedule and see instructions) | | | | | | |
| 12 | **Unusual grants** | | | | | | |
| 13 | Total Revenue Add lines 10 through 12 | | | | | | |
| **Expenses** | | | | | | | |
| 14 | Fundraising expenses | | | | | | |
| 15 | Contributions, gifts, grants, and similar amounts paid out (attach an itemized list) | | | | | | |
| 16 | Disbursements to or for the benefit of members (attach an itemized list) | | | | | | |
| 17 | Compensation of officers, directors, and trustees | | | | | | |
| 18 | Other salaries and wages | | | | | | |
| 19 | Interest expense | | | | | | |
| 20 | Occupancy (rent, utilities, etc.) | | | | | | |
| 21 | Depreciation and depletion | | | | | | |
| 22 | Professional fees | | | | | | |
| 23 | Any expense not otherwise classified, such as program services (attach itemized list) | | | | | | |
| 24 | Total Expenses Add lines 14 through 23 | | | | | | |

Form **1023** (Rev. 12-2013)

## X. CONFLICT OF INTEREST

This subject was mentioned earlier. The IRS frowns upon an all family board of officers, board members, staff, volunteers who provide business services to the NFP in which they serve. It is important to avoid self-gain.

You cannot lease properties to family members. Also, a conflict of interest would be if other organizations are coming in to do fundraisers, operate and sell goods to your organization. Hence, board members cannot profit through the NFP; although, they may have a FP business.

## XI. NON-PROFIT TAX REPORTING

Here is where confusion comes into play. A NFP is considered a corporation business; however, a 501(c)(3) organization is exempt from paying state and federal taxes. The staff of the NFP is still responsible to report during the tax season to the IRS. The reporting is totally different from domestic and foreign corporations. The NFPs are required to either complete a 990, 990EZ, or 990E-Post Card like completing 1040s. However, what is being reported are the funds that came into the NFP for that fiscal calendar year. For example, if an organization receives over $50,000 in donations, a 990 long hard copy form needs to be completed and submitted. There is the short form 990EZ to use if the focus is only monetary contributions. The long forms are used when you are reporting monetary contributions, properties, arts, etc. If the contribution is less than $50,000 for the 501(c)(3) NFP, the 990E-Post Card needs to be completed online.

These reports must be filed five (5) months after their fiscal year by the 15th day of that month. If your NFP fiscal year ends in December, you need to file the appropriate 990 by May 15th. So far, there are no late fees. <u>Please note</u>: **Since 2010, a ruling was passed that if you missed three (3) consecutive years of filings, the 501(c)(3) will be revoked.** Once again it is very important that you periodically check IRS.gov website for new rulings under public charities that will affect NFPs.

**When the NFP is a 501(c)(3) organization who is required to file taxes?**

_______________________________________________________________

_______________________________________________________________

_______________________________________________________________

_______________________________________________________________

**What do NFPs have to report?** _______________________________

_______________________________________________________________

_______________________________________________________________

_______________________________________________________________

**What can cause your 501(c)(3) to be revoked?** _______________________

_______________________________________________________________

_______________________________________________________________

_______________________________________________________________

## XII.  CHURCHES/OTHERS

Churches are required to submit additional information along with the above information.

Churches are required to submit a tenet of faith, church constitution in addition to church Bylaws, a copy of the lease or proof of ownership of the building, pictures of the sanctuary, printed programs of service, organizational chart, church history, church programs, requirement for Ordination, ministerial leadership training programs, an established weekly Sunday school, membership requirements, and sacrament functions.

Every church is expected to submit a Tenet of Faith which is according to their belief. For example, if the church is Christian based, Protestant, Methodist, etc., the language must appear in the Tenet of Faith. Accordingly, if it is a Christian Church, you believe in the trinity, water baptism, communion, and the Old and New Testament.

The church constitution is like the United States Constitution. In your church constitution you are explaining the makeup, structure, principles, arrangement and formation. It also gives the concepts and character of what the church is all about. If the church owns its building, a copy of the deed will have to be submitted to the IRS. If the church is leasing space, a copy of the lease agreement must be submitted to the IRS. The IRS also requires that you take outside and inside pictures of the church building where worship is conducted.

The IRS would also like for you to include in your application a printed program of your services. Most churches submit their Sunday bulletin that reflects the order of service, and the announcements of bible studies, and other functions and events of the churches.

In addition, the IRS would like an organizational chart which lists the chain of command within the church. To be considered for the tax-exempt status for the 501(c)(3), the church must have a board, a pastor, and others listed within the organizational chart. You can also use this chart as a diagram to list the various auxiliaries within the church and the leadership department head who oversees each auxiliary within the church, such as: Deacon and Deaconess Boards, Trustee Board, Praise Team, Missionary Board, Food Ministry, Music Ministry, Usher Board, etc.

The IRS also wants information regarding your church's history. Most churches submit their programs when they host a church anniversary, or they have the history written as a separate document. It is required to list every program that is provided (*e.g.*, Sunday School, Morning Worship, Evening Services, Bible Study, Women's Day, Men's Day, Pastor's Anniversary, Choir Anniversary, events, etc.). Include information regarding the spiritual leader and his/her credentials are required for submission as well. The church is required to have a training program for future ministers. The future ministers are required to complete an application, pay an application fee, take a course of study, and complete the exam.

You also must report the candidate's first sermon, meetings with the board, and ordinations along with documentation. Each candidate should have a folder and you should have a copy of the curriculum as well. In addition, your church must have a Sunday school for the young and perform sacrament services to qualify for the 501(c)(3) tax-exempt service.

You can have all the above and exclude Sunday school for the young and the sacrament services and you will be declined. You would be surprised that there are some churches that do not have Sunday school. That is a NO, NO.

What is a sacrament service? Do you conduct weddings? Do you conduct funerals? Do you conduct burials? Do you provide communion? You must provide the above services for the 501(c)(3) determination. In addition, the IRS will want to know your membership count and a number of those that show up for services. They will also want to know if the members are permitted to be a part of another ministry. It is required to explain how people can become members of your church.

Are the members required to fill out an application? Are they required to attend a new member's class? Do they have to confess Christ? Are they required to sign a creed to accept membership rules? If so, you must have a measure of discipline. What happens when a member does not conduct themselves as expected? Are they removed from the membership? If so, what is that process to remove them from the membership?

In addition, there is what is known as schedules within the application that churches must provide. You must complete those schedules by answering questions. Example of the questions can range from how many members do the church have? Are members permitted to be members of other churches? Does the church have a minister? And other related questions. Once all the above is addressed, you are ready to submit the 501(c)(3) application.

There are schools, civic centers, lodges, and others that seek the 501(c)(3) determination. What is required is that you complete all twelve (12) pages of the application and the corresponding appropriate schedules for your organization. Schedules are additional forms to list added information that has been requested. Every NFP does not have to submit schedules. Most common ones that do have to submit schedules are churches, daycare centers, housing, and others along with their applications.

**Q:** Who does your NFP belong to?

**A:**

**Q:** Once you file your NFP with the state and on the federal level, is it important to file with the Attorney General's Office?

**A:**

**Q:** What is an EIN?

**A:**

## NFP OTHER

### I. CHARITABLE POLICY

You are required to have a charitable policy. A charitable policy is a statement that you do not discriminate against a person due to race, age, ethnicity, etc. In addition, list the target population for whom you have and will serve. This charitable policy comes in handy when it's time to request the sales tax-exemption.

### II. ATTORNEY GENERAL OFFICE

Every state has an attorney general's office. Most NFPs, once incorporated and receive the 501(c)(3) determination from the IRS, rarely register with the attorney general's office. Why?

Because the board is unaware or do not deem it necessary and feel that if the NFP is recognized on both the state and federal level as a NFP, that should be sufficient. However, that is not enough. It is a mandate to be registered with the attorney general's office. You must request a registration form in the State where your NFP resides. You can complete a CO1 and a CO2. If you are a church, you are to complete a CO3.

CO is an abbreviation for charitable organization. Once you are registered, you are placed in the Attorney General's database. Funders check this database to see if you are registered as well as Jesse White's office or the office in the state which you are registered and the IRS database. Failure to register with the Attorney General's office can result in a penalty especially if you collected funds prior to registration. People have paid stiff penalties up to $10,000 or more for receiving donations and not being registered. You must register with the Attorney General's office of your state in which the NFP resides.

## III. THE DEPARTMENT OF REVENUE

The Department of Revenue is the department to contact when seeking the sales tax-exemption. There is no fee for the sales tax-exemption. However, make sure that you have reached the sales tax division for NFP.

There is a division that handles domestic corporations and you want to be exempt from taxes, so you must make sure that you have the right department. (First, you must know that the 501(c)(3) determination letter exempts the donations that are given to the NFP from state and federal taxes.) The 501(c)(3) determination letter does not exempt the NFP from sales taxes. However, the sales tax-exemption letter allows you to not pay taxes on merchandise. The document that exempts NFP from sales taxes comes from the Department of Revenue and every state has that department.

In Illinois the number issued starts with a letter. Once that document is attained, any purchases on behalf of the organization can be exempt from sales taxes. The document can be used to purchase household items, personal hygienic items, cars, properties, etc. sales tax free. If you do conferences, rent facilities, or make purchases, you can obtain sales tax free as well.

What is required? You can apply online or in writing. When applying on-line, just give the required information. If you apply in writing you must submit a letter; brochure that includes days and hours of operation, services provided, charitable policy, and eligibility requirements for services; a copy of the article of incorporation, and the 501(c)(3). If you are a church, pictures and a copy of your lease or copy of your deed must be included.

**How many ways can you apply for sales tax-exemption? And what are they?**

_______________________________________________________________

_______________________________________________________________

_______________________________________________________________

_______________________________________________________________

**If you are a church, what are some of the items you need to submit when applying for sales tax-exemption?** _______________________________________

_______________________________________________________________

_______________________________________________________________

_______________________________________________________________

## IV. BUSINESS REGISTRATION

You are required to register your business with your state's Department of Revenue. You can do it online by downloading the form, complete it, and mail in the form to your state Department of Revenue.

## V. BUSINESS LICENSE

Usually NFPs are not required to have business licenses unless products are being sold. Selling merchandise requires a license. For example, some NFPs have vending machines or a coffee café. If that is the case, you are required to have a license because the income that was generated is not tax-free.

**Are NFPs required to have a business license?**

Yes _______ No _______

## VI. DUN & BRADSTREET

There is a nine-digit identification number to identify your business whether it is a NFP or an FP. This is used to set up a credit profile that lenders and potential partners can review to assess the financial stability of your organization. If you intend to apply for governmental grants, it is mandatory to have this number. If you are a

NFP that is applying for governmental grants, it is mandatory that you have what is referred to as a DUNs number. The DUNs number is free.

**Is it required to have a DUNs number when operating a NFP?** Yes ___ or No __

**Why is it important to have a DUNs number?** _______________________________

_______________________________________________________________

_______________________________________________________________

_______________________________________________________________

## VII.    SAM

If you intend to be a federal contractor, in addition to the DUNs number, you will need a SAM number; which stands for system award management number. You must apply if planning to submit federal grants. The SAM number is free.

**What are some businesses that you can add to the NFP?**

_______________________________________________________________

_______________________________________________________________

_______________________________________________________________

_______________________________________________________________

_______________________________________________________________

_______________________________________________________________

**Do you have to file taxes on the money you make in the business(es)?**
Yes _______ or No ________

## VIII.    UNRELATED BUSINESS ACTIVITIES

There are many NFPs that have businesses that generate income and use revenues to support their mission and to continue to provide services. A good example is the Salvation Army. We know their mission is human services, and the organization provides housing, clothing, and shelter. However, they are well known for their thrift stores which is a business that generates revenue to support their services. Catholic Charities provides social services, yet they have day care centers, which is a business. Churches and ministries provide bookstores, restaurants, cafés, day care centers, schools, messenger services, etc. that generates business.

In the above cases, business licenses are required, and the income must be reported on the 990 as unrelated business. What does unrelated business mean? It means that the NFP has this activity to raise funding for their mission, but this activity has nothing to do with the NFP mission. There is a section on the 990 to do the reporting of unrelated business.

Of course, taxes must be paid on the state and federal level because those profits are not exempt nor covered by the 501(c)(3).

## IX. SUSTAINABILITY

NFPs must be ready to develop a sustainability plan, especially when it's time to seek funding for program activities. Long gone are the endless years of funding.

Foundations do not want to be deemed an ATM machine nor NFP welfare system. In other words, the 501(c)(3) covers charitable activities. Charitable means FREE services that are supported by grants, private donations, sponsorship, contributions, and fundraising distributed to the target population.

For example, if you have a youth program and the children are receiving tutoring, mentoring, seminars and workshops, but you host a skating party and charge a fee, the skating party has nothing to do with tutoring, mentoring, seminars, or workshops. The skating party is not related to the reason that the NFP was formed. Anywhere that you are charging a price for an event, it is an unrelated activity to the NFP's mission.

Funders want to provide funding on a short-term scenario, therefore, they are expecting NFPs to have a plan that if they decide not to fund the NFP that the services will not discontinue. In the NFP arena, Funders are requesting sustainability programs. Funding can be for one

(1) year, two (2) years, three (3) years, and even five (5) years. Some grants are a one-time deal. Other grants you may have to renew through the grant application process annually. The length of how long a NFP can receive funding from a grant maker is determined by the funder. Whatever the case, a plan to sustain services need to be developed.

Some NFPs invest funds that they receive into the stock market. It is legal to do so. How do you think the Catholic Church obtained such huge massive wealth although it's now drying up due to the various lawsuits that they have acquired?

I do not remember which pope, but there was a pope that had a secret meeting with JP Morgan and he handed over several chests filled with contributions not knowing what to do with it. Well, JP Morgan took the funds back in the 1700s and this financial wizard made that denomination rich.

Some NFPs open businesses that generate income to fund program services. A perfect example, the arts and multicultural centers charge for performances and give lessons. Some NFPs form community gardens and sell vegetables to generate funds. Some NFPs secure properties and rent space in homes and offices to generate funding. There are others that open stores, daycare centers, bookstores, cafés, coffee shops, and the list goes on and on. One must do an assessment and determine how to generate funding inside and outside of the NFP. We are living in times where Funders are asking for the secure sustainability plans to be submitted along with proposals.

**What are some of the ways you plan to sustain the NFP?**

_______________________________________________________________

_______________________________________________________________

_______________________________________________________________

_______________________________________________________________

_______________________________________________________________

**Why is it important?** _______________________________________

_______________________________________________

_______________________________________________

_______________________________________________

_______________________________________________

## X. COLLABORATIVE ACTIVITIES

The days of the "long rangers" are over. The "long rangers" are those who come to rescue you when your plan does not work. Funders are looking for NFPs to pull their resources together and many grants require multiple NFPs to appear inside the grants. However, NFPs must protect themselves with a Memorandum of Understanding because in the past, NFPs received funding that did not pay out to the others on the grant.

In Closing, now you have explored the possibility of setting up a NFP. Hopefully, the information will jolt and jumpstart you. But guess what? You must now learn how to operate and manage your NFP after the startup phase.

**What is a Memorandum of Understanding?** _______________________________

_______________________________________________

_______________________________________________

You thought that was it? NO. You are only just beginning. Here are some other items to consider.

## XI. LIABILITY INSURANCE

Every NFP need liability insurances for several reasons. If someone falls or you are involved in an accident, you will have coverage. The board members and staff need to be covered under liability insurance in case erroneous advice is given to clients or some type of harm is caused by the people that represent the organization. Lastly, most Funders want to know if the NFP is covered with liability so that the grant monies will not be a resource to deal with liabilities or lawsuits. If your

NFP has a DBA clause (Doing Business As) which creates an FP, coverage will be needed to qualify for bid opportunities with businesses and governmental entities.

**Why does a NFP need liability insurance?** _______________________________

_______________________________________________________

_______________________________________________________

## XII.    BROCHURES/STATIONERY/BUSINESS CARDS

Some people jump the gun when it comes to this topic. You should not have business cards, postcards, brochures printed until you are incorporated. I have met people that were not incorporated who had brochures, business cards, and postcards printed while they were working toward becoming legitimate. Others felt that it was too much work and fees to legalize themselves and chose to continue with the business as usual. Once again, if you are operating a NFP and are not incorporated by your secretary of state, and not registered with your state's attorney general office, you can be shut down and receive huge fines. Once you are incorporated, you can proceed to develop, and print your brochures, business cards, and the like whether you have the 501(c)(3) determination or not. Remember, the 501(c)(3) is for tax-exempt purposes.

**When is it a great time to print business materials?**

_______________________________________________________

_______________________________________________________

_______________________________________________________

## XIII.    WEBSITE/SOCIAL MEDIA

Once you are incorporated, you can move forward to hiring a web designer or develop your own web design through self-help. You can google, and sites will come up with do it yourself templates. In addition, you can also find companies that will assist you in designing your website for a nominal fee. Vistaprint is a well-known established company that specializes in helping startups. Wix.com offers free websites if you are willing to advertise their name. However, the company appears to be more legitimate when the web address does not include wix.com in the address. Therefore, pay the annual fee. Many NFPs as well as FPs have set up Facebook pages to offer their programs, services, and products.

## XIV. PAYROLL

Once you have everything set up, you need employees. There will come a time where you will need full time staff or part time. Once you start issuing pay checks, although, the NFP is exempt from paying state and federal taxes, the employees are not tax-exempt. You are responsible for what is known as FICA. You will have to have employees fill-out a W-4 to take out state and federal taxes, and social security. There are a few other taxes from employees' paychecks and it must be the correct amount or employees will have to pay taxes. You must do your research and stay abreast as tax laws requirements change from time to time. It is to your advantage to hire a bookkeeper, hire an accountant, or a CPA to handle this task. You can have the option of using software that automatically issues payroll checks and make deductions. Or you can rely upon your bank or a company that specialize in offering payroll services. Whatever the case, you must make sure that the taxes arrive on time (quarterly) or you will be hit with a hefty fine.

**What are good software systems to use for payroll?**

___________________________________________________________

___________________________________________________________

___________________________________________________________

___________________________________________________________

___________________________________________________________

## XV. ADDITIONAL ITEMS

Below is a list of information to implement in your NFP:

- Policies & Procedures,
- Grievance policy,
- Program record keeping,

- Fiscal record keeping,
- Workman compensation,
- Unemployment insurance,
- Job Titles,
- Job Descriptions,
- Applications,
- Background checks,
- Credit checks,
- Drug tests,
- Resource development,
- Employee evaluations,
- Ordering Equipment & Supplies,
- Staff Development,
- Department of Labor Laws & Wages Assignments, and
- A host of other things.

## DIVISION II – RESOURCE DEVELOPMENT

Alrighty! I do not want you to feel overwhelmed regarding the above information. I have decided to break the Resource Development into topics to make it easier for you to navigate.

I will cover private contributors and other helpful information. Monetary donations, party planning, volunteer recruitment, social media how the networks can be used to create campaigns for funding, crowd funding, and Banks. We will also cover grant writing formats, different types of grants, the Letter of Intent, Standard Grant Proposal, along with logging online to fill-out grant applications, grant research, grant proposal checklist, and Funders.

Take a sigh. Now, let's dive-in.

Usually, once an organization becomes incorporated, 501c3 status, Bylaws governed with all the other trimmings, it never fails everyone is now hyped and ready to solicit for grants. Right? Wrong. Due to the economy, and Funders a/k/a grant makers cut backs, it is now very competitive to obtain grants.

Imagine a pie in the 1960s-1990s grants were 90% of the pie. Now it is only 10% of the pie. The organization in which you operate must now be resourceful, innovative, creative, and inventive in order to deliver your program services. You must now rely upon resource development.

## DEFINITION OF RESOURCES

What is resource development? Resource development is to assess what is needed and then seek out those resources or rather the goods needed to supply and meet the need whether monetary or non-monetary. You can no longer depend on a grant only to help your organization to operate and provide services to your target population.

What is resource development?

_____________________________________

_____________________________________

_____________________________________

_____________________________________

_____________________________________

Why should an organization seek out grants through other resources?

_____________________________________

_____________________________________

_____________________________________

_____________________________________

_____________________________________

_____________________________________

Make a list of items that your organization needs for startup
(*i.e.*, office supplies, computers, etc.)

_____________________________________

_____________________________________

_____________________________________

_____________________________________

_____________________________________

_____________________________________

_____________________________________

_____________________________________

Make a list of companies that has those items that you can contact for donations.

_________________________________________________

_________________________________________________

_________________________________________________

_________________________________________________

_________________________________________________

_________________________________________________

_________________________________________________

_________________________________________________

Now, it would be great if NFPs could search through google or take recommendations and **develop a partnership, collaboration, networking base effort with another NFP that has history in the funding world**. Those established NFPs have the options of issuing grants to smaller NFPs or be included in the future grant writing process. And for those that do not have the 501(c)(3) IRS status but your NFP is recognized by the state in which the NFP resides, **the established NFP can serve as a fiscal 501(c)(3) sponsor agent for your organization.** What does that mean? You can write grants and list them upon approval that they will handle the funds on behalf of your organization and make sure the goals of the grants are met. There is an advantage and disadvantage of having a fiscal 501(c)(3) sponsor. The advantage is Funders are more likely to consider you for funding if you are under an established well-known organization. The down-side you can become a dependent and will not seek your own 501(c)(3), and lastly you have absolutely no control of the funds.

Microsoft is a great resource to tap into. The company gives away to NFPs free software and they even help develop software. The company offers training in Microsoft to your staff. They have even been known to do onsite training at NFPs for a class of ten (10) or more. In addition, there are grants that NFPs can apply for with Microsoft.

Lastly, Google the following organizations that provide training, funding, or link you to Funders, workshops, and other resources that may be pertinent to your NFP and many of them have grant programs as well:

- ArtistShare
- Chicago Artist Resources
- Resource Hubs/Incubators
- Women Business Development Center
- Legal Assistance
- Score
- Small Business Administration (SBA)
- University of Chicago (community programs accelerator)
- Heartland Payment Systems
- Chamber of Commerce

In addition, Funders are expecting you to have a funding history, the ability to partner with other organizations, share resources, and you are expected to have a sustainability program. The Funders expect your organization and its programs to continue functioning if they decide to cease from providing their support. Your organization will need to explore social enterprises and/or sustainability projects.

Social enterprise involves your NFP setting up an actual business that will generate revenues that can be channeled back into the NFP. A great example will be the Salvation Army, which has a For-Profit that is a thrift store. When you do a social enterprise, it is considered an unrelated business to appear on the 990-tax return. The NFP can have a business.

Now, if you want to do something periodically, then you can from time to time develop sustainability projects that may be seasonal of items to be sold, that too will have to appear on the 990 as unrelated businesses.

A social enterprise can be set up in three ways: (i) contact IRS for a specific form for your NFP that will allow you to have a D/B/A (Doing Business As). The business name will be different from the NFP. You must also do the paperwork on the state and city level by contacting the municipal business offices, (ii) your social enterprise can also be listed as an unrelated business on the organization's 990 Form, and (iii) you can just set up a For-Profit business corporation or LLC separate from the NFP and report taxes annually as required.

**BELOW ARE COMMON BUSINESSES SET UP BY NFPS:**

- Day cares,
- Adult day cares,
- Book stores,
- Cafés,
- Thrift stores,
- Landscaping,
- Cleaning services,
- Tax services, and
- Messenger services.

There are other social enterprises. The list above is just several for you to consider.

Whenever our country has a new federal governmental administration, the game always changes. Keep track, continue researching, and reviewing the IRS website (irs.gov) to stay abreast to the different changes.

1. What is a funding history?

_______________________________________________
_______________________________________________
_______________________________________________
_______________________________________________
_______________________________________________

2. How do you put together a funding history?

_______________________________________________
_______________________________________________
_______________________________________________
_______________________________________________
_______________________________________________

3. What is a sustainability program?  Why are Funders requiring that organizations have a sustainability program?

_______________________________________________
_______________________________________________
_______________________________________________
_______________________________________________
_______________________________________________

4.  Make a list of three venues that can aide in a sustainability program for your organization:

    a.  ________________________________________

    b.  ________________________________________

    c.  ________________________________________

# RESOURCES FOR NFP

## I.   PRIVATE CONTRIBUTORS AND OTHERS

The first thing you should do prior to asking anybody for funding is to do an internal assessment.  What do your organization need? Do you need office equipment? Office supplies? Office furnishings? What is needed?  Do you need monetary contributions? You should then make a list and think who would be able to donate those items. Have an open mind for refurbish items, although, some may give brand new items.  Shift through **your** closets to find some items that you can use for your sustainability program. Ask **family members** and even **board members** if they have anything that can be added. List those items as Inkind donations.

InKind donations are items that are nonmonetary (NO DOLLARS). The **InKind donations** can meet the needs in place of money donations.

### INKIND DONATIONS:

List Inkind Donations from Family, Friends, Neighbors, Co-workers, and Others:

1.  ________________________________________________

2.  ________________________________________________

3.  ________________________________________________

4.  ________________________________________________

5.  ________________________________________________

6.  ________________________________________________

7.  ________________________________________________

8. _______________________________________________

9. _______________________________________________

10. ______________________________________________

11. ______________________________________________

12. ______________________________________________

13. ______________________________________________

14. ______________________________________________

15. ______________________________________________

16. ______________________________________________

17. ______________________________________________

18. ______________________________________________

19. ______________________________________________

20. ______________________________________________

## II.  MONETARY DONATIONS

Now, when you need monetary contributions, make a list of every family member eighteen (18) years and above, **friends, neighbors,** and **everyone that you have done business with.** Let's say you have a community closet, you can seek **donations from cleaners at the end of the year** to fill your organization's closet program. **Think about what is needed for the organization and the programs of the organization.** Contact everyone that always remembers your **birthdays, anniversaries,** and **holidays** use that money.

Throw a birthday shower/party for your NFP. Yes. You read right. When we usually throw a birthday party for ourselves or someone does it for us, what happens? People bring gifts. The gifts are either monetary or nonmonetary. You can send a wish list to make things easier for your soon to be Donors. Have food, beverages, music and lots of fun. You should have two lists to record all donations whether monetary or nonmonetary. Record the name, item, dollar amount and of course the date. This will help you put together a funding history. Any monies that you contribute make sure you list yourself as a donor as well.

You can also offer membership opportunities where people give donations to be a member of your NFP; however, the membership must be listed in the NFP organizing document (Articles of Incorporation) and within the NFP Bylaws as well. Design a membership package that is inviting. Most people care about others and will want to be part of the NFP.

Here is an example, museums offer memberships that are paid annually. The members that pay annually are offered several benefits compared to those who are non-members.

Incorporate the information above only if your NFP will have a membership signup and package. There are some NFPs that do not offer memberships.

You can develop a volunteer pool to assist you with what is about to be shared. How do you go about obtaining volunteers? Check out volunteermatch.com, church members, and others who would not mind donating a couple of hours per week in **phone solicitation**, **mailing solicitation**, and even **canvassing** to obtain monetary donations. You can also post flyers asking for volunteers, and put announcements in church bulletins.

You can use **emails** to seek contributions. There are companies that you can **buy emails** from with the purpose of seeking donations. Your organization's website can have a **donation button** on it, and other **organizations that you have a relationship with can also have a link or a donation button on their site for your NFP as well.**

Speaking of websites, you can use **social media or develop a page for your organization on Facebook, LinkedIn, and other social media websites.**

**Every Thanksgiving and Christmas the Salvation Army is known for their volunteers and red kettle in front of major stores**

**ringing their bells for donations.  You can also get your kettle of a different color and find stores that have preapproved you to stand in front of and ring your bell.**

In addition, we have all shopped at grocery stores, cleaners, gas stations, 7-Elevens and other stores where **jars are at the cash register, so people can give donations (coins and/or bills).**  Matter of a fact, have **a large jar in a secure place so that staff, volunteers, clients, visitors, and all others can periodically drop their change in the jar onsite of your NFP. You can also have a place to receive donations of any amounts.** Look for sites to leave containers for donations.

List five (5) grocery stores to contact their corporate office for donations:

1.__________________________________________________

2.__________________________________________________

3.__________________________________________________

4.__________________________________________________

5.__________________________________________________

List five (5) Cleaners (If your program has a distribution component):

1.__________________________________________________

2.__________________________________________________

3.__________________________________________________

4.__________________________________________________

5.__________________________________________________

List 5 Gas Stations:

1.__________________________________________________

2.__________________________________________________

3.__________________________________________________

4.__________________________________________________

5.___________________________________________

Create a list of potential sponsors:

1.___________________________________________

2.___________________________________________

3.___________________________________________

4.___________________________________________

5.___________________________________________

6.___________________________________________

7.___________________________________________

8.___________________________________________

9.___________________________________________

10.___________________________________________

List Three (3) possible Annual Events (*i.e.,* Gala Dinners, Cake Walks, and/or Picnics)

1. ___________________________________________
2. ___________________________________________
3. ___________________________________________

List ideas that can evolve into annual events for your organization then select one and hold a planning session with the board, staff, and volunteers:

1. ___________________________________________
2. ___________________________________________
3. ___________________________________________

## III.     ALDERMAN/COUNCILMAN

I am now going to share what a lot of people do not know. Your alderman, state representatives, and other officials many times have cash inside their offices to use for causes. Cause means, petty cash A/K/A kitty that can be used to fund community projects and give out scholarships.

How do you think the block clubs have parties, and other events occur for communities?

**List your Alderman/Councilman contact information:**

_______________________________

_______________________________

_______________________________

_______________________________

_______________________________

_______________________________

_______________________________

_______________________________

_______________________________

_______________________________

**List your State Representative contact information:**

_______________________________

_______________________________

_______________________________

_______________________________

_______________________________

**List your State Senator contact information:**

_______________________________________

_______________________________________

_______________________________________

_______________________________________

_______________________________________

**List your City County Commissioner contact information:**

_______________________________________

_______________________________________

_______________________________________

_______________________________________

_______________________________________

## IV.    OTHER RESOURCES

Another resource is, once you have the NFP startup with all NFP documentations and a bank account, **why not ask YOUR bank.** Some families have been banking with a certain bank for many years. Why not ask that bank to contribute toward your NFP? **Seek out the personal banker, CRA Officer, or VP of the bank to request a donation reminding them how long you and your family have been banking with them. You would reach out to them with a Letter of Intent which is covered in Division III** of this book and make an appointment and take the letter in to them personally. **Then move on to other local banks that are around your NFP then broaden your reach to others.** Let everybody know who has contributed to your NFP, and they will be more than happy to contribute as well. Also, obtain a listing of **businesses around the NFP and beyond and request donations from**

**them as well.** In some cases, you will be referred to their corporate offices. Some will only give InKind donations, others monetary donations, and then you have those that will provide both donations.

Please issue a THANK YOU CARD to your Donors. If donations are $250 or more, then that donation is tax-exempt. For more details, contact the IRS and, also, inquire about the non-monetary donation items at irs.gov.

It is important that you stay abreast of what is happening in your neighborhood and even outside of your neighborhood. Keep your ears and eyes open for any **school closings or businesses that are closing**. More often than none, **schools and businesses are looking to get rid of merchandise to update anywhere from free to a very small nominal fee**. Contact them as soon as possible once you find out. **Many will donate because they can get a tax write-off in lieu of sales which is just as good.**

Another resource is to seek out **sponsors for your programs, seasonal and annual events that your organization may have during the year.** You would issue them a sponsorship letter explaining why they are being contacted, the program service that needs to be sponsored, and how they could benefit in being the organization's sponsor.

The following are some of what you can offer sponsors: (1) speaking time at your event, (2) an event table, (3) priority seating, (4) VIP treatment, (5) a listing in your program, (6) a copy of the sign in list, or (7) a program and/or building named after them. Just be creative in what you will be offering in exchange for their sponsorship.

All NFPs should have an **annual fundraising event**. A lot of NFPs host galas, dinners, or party themes to raise funds for their NFP. The annual and even a quarterly event could be **bake goods, cake walks, dance competitions, etc. Whatever you come up with, make sure that tickets state the word DONATION.**

There have been organizations that have been investigated and some causes loss their 501c3 status because they did not use the word **DONATION. If you do not use the word donation than whatever you collect is viewed as a profit by the IRS and taxes must be paid.** Now, there are still NFPs that rely upon fundraising projects such as cookies, candies, candles, and even donuts to bring in donations. You can also consider that as well.

Keep in mind that when creating your fundraisers, do not use the word sale, fees, price, or costs. The focus should be on fundraising. It is best to say donations and contributions. Hence, otherwise, you will have to pay taxes on any items sold.

Your NFP can develop **training programs or products that can be listed in Groupon** which will generate funding for the NFP, seek out a representative for additional information at www.groupon.com.

Fund Drive is another organization that assists NFPs in raising funds by encouraging the staff of the NFP to set up drives onsite. The drive usually consists of gently worn clothes, appliances, etc. However, it is best to obtain a vast amount. Some have been known to raise anywhere from \$100 to \$1,000. You and the staff of Fund Drive will set the fundraising goal. The staff of the Fund Drive also helps with the advertisement, setup, and more.

Make a list of ten (10) companies to contact for monetary donations:

| Company's Name | Company's Address/Phone no. | Company's Response |
|---|---|---|
| 1. | | |
| 2. | | |
| 3. | | |

| Company's Name | Company's Address/Phone no. | Company's Response |
| --- | --- | --- |
| 4. | | |
| 5. | | |
| 6. | | |
| 7. | | |
| 8. | | |
| 9. | | |
| 10. | | |

## V.   BUDGETING

Create an organizational budget (A/K/A agency budget). Please review the organizational budget in the NFP section of Division I of this book.

Have a budget for each program service that you are providing. How much will it cost to operate your program? Program services such as cooking classes, community outreach, senior activities, food pantry, and activities that will benefit the public. The benefit of budgeting a program is to present to a funder whenever you may seek funding for programs. The budget will already be in place. The budget also may be to your benefit so that you will stay within the budget.

For example,
- The cost to rent,
- Phone,
- Salary,
- Equipment,
- Venue,
- Classes,
- Food, and
- Transportation.

## VI.   PLAN NFP BIRTHDAY SHOWER/PARTY

The benefit of having a birthday shower/party was mentioned earlier. Below is a list of what you can use when organizing the birthday shower/party.

Date:

Time:

Place:

Attire:

Invite:

Refreshments:

Music:

Program:

Other:

## VII.   VOLUNTEER RECRUITMENT PLAN

A NFP startup has a board of directors, then staff which may consist of a couple of full time employees and part time employees. However, the backbone of the NFPs are the volunteers that serve. A volunteer recruitment plan consists of, but are not limited to, recruiting people who are usually unemployed, underemployed, college students, etc., who are looking to acquire skills, update skills, trainings, job leads and even recommendations to companies in which they may be employed. A lot of NFPs oftentimes hire from their volunteer pool, because they are familiar with the organization, policies and procedures, the target population which are the people they serve on behalf of the NFPs. Most times volunteers that have been trained within the same field of your organization will have the experience necessary to assist your NFP.

A good source of volunteers would be seniors, retirees, veterans, and stay at home moms whose children are now in school on a fulltime basis.  NFPs should also consider recruiting professional volunteers as well.  The startups should seek people that can serve as a volunteer such as a lawyer, accountant, project manager, technical adviser. The volunteers can serve as outreach workers, food distributors, coordinators, and others.  The NFPs must determine the job titles based on their programs.

1.   Make a list of places to recruit potential volunteers involved with churches, schools, residents of the community, unemployment office, etc.

_________________________________________________

_________________________________________________

_________________________________________________

_________________________________________________

_________________________________________________

_________________________________________________

________________________________________________

________________________________________________

________________________________________________

________________________________________________

________________________________________________

________________________________________________

________________________________________________

2. Have potential volunteers fill-out an application. The following is a Sample Volunteer Application from Strengthening Non-Profits:

Application Date _______________

Volunteer Position Sought

________________________________________________

Name ___________________________________________

Home Address ___________________________________

Work Phone _______________Home Phone ____________________

**EDUCATION**

Highest Level of Education

________________________________________________

________________________________________________

________________________________________________

**EMPLOYMENT**

Current Employer, if applicable:

Position/Title

________________________________________________

Dates of Employment (starting, ending)

________________________________________________

Company/Employer

________________________________________________

Address

________________________________________________

Would you like us to keep your employer abreast of your volunteer service and achievement?  No ☐ Yes ☐

## SKILLS & EXPERIENCE

Special training, skills, hobbies

_______________________________________________________________

Groups, clubs, organizational memberships

_______________________________________________________________

Please describe your prior volunteer experience (include organization names and dates of service)

_______________________________________________________________

_______________________________________________________________

_______________________________________________________________

_______________________________________________________________

What experiences have you had that may prepare you to work as a volunteer in the field of [description of field, *e.g.*, domestic violence, child abuse prevention, youth recreation, etc.]?

_______________________________________________________________

_______________________________________________________________

_______________________________________________________________

Why do you want to volunteer? [Or, what do you want to gain from this volunteer experience?]

_______________________________________________________________

_______________________________________________________________

_______________________________________________________________

_______________________________________________________________

Have you ever been convicted of a crime? [If yes, please explain the nature of the crime and the date of the conviction and disposition.] Conviction of a crime is not an automatic disqualification for volunteer work.

_______________________________________________________________

_______________________________________________________________

_______________________________________________________________

Do you have a driver's license? No ☐ Yes ☐
Do you have car insurance? No ☐ Yes ☐
Do you have a car available for transporting others? No ☐ Yes ☐

## REFERENCES

Please list three people who know you well and can attest to your character, skills, and dependability. Include your current or last employer.

| Name/Organization | Relationship to you | Length of relationship | Phone number |
| --- | --- | --- | --- |
| _________ | _________ | _________ | _________ |
| _________ | _________ | _________ | _________ |
| _________ | _________ | _________ | _________ |

______________  ______________  ______________  ______________

______________  ______________  ______________  ______________

______________  ______________  ______________  ______________

______________  ______________  ______________  ______________

______________  ______________  ______________  ______________

______________  ______________  ______________  ______________

**Please read the following carefully before signing this application:**

I understand that this is an application for and not a commitment or promise of volunteer opportunity. I certify that I have and will provide information throughout the selection process, including on this application for a volunteer position and in interviews with **[Name of Nonprofit]** that is true, correct and complete to the best of my knowledge. I certify that I have and will answer all questions to the best of my ability and that I have not and will not withhold any information that would unfavorably affect my application for a volunteer position. I understand that information contained on my application will be verified by **[Name of Nonprofit]**. I understand that misrepresentations or omissions may be cause for my immediate rejection as an applicant for a volunteer position with **[Name of Nonprofit]** or my termination as a volunteer.

Signature ___________________________________________ Date ____________

Print Name: _________________________________________________

3.  Follow up on responses.
4.  Interview potential volunteers. Here are some questions to ask the volunteers: (a) Tell me about yourself; (b) Why did you signup to volunteer; (c) What would you like to offer to the community; (d) What are your skill set; (e) What is your area of expertise? and (f) What position would you best serve in? Come up with questions that will best fit your NFP organization.
5.  Hold an orientation that consist of, (a) the organization's mission and vision statements, (b) organizational chart and the chain of command, (c) protocols, (d) volunteers' job titles and job descriptions, (e) the benefits of volunteering, and (f) upcoming required classes to be taken prior to volunteering.
6.  Provide training for the volunteers such as communication and training on assignments.

7. Food menu for volunteers. Whenever you hold a meeting there should be some type of refreshments present for the volunteers which will show that they are important to you and to spread some cheer. It is based on your organization's budget, the food that will be served. You can have light refreshments such as pastries and bake goods along with various juices and coffees or you can do finger sandwiches, chips, along with juices, bottled water, sodas or you can cater perhaps from a vendor like Jimmy Johns, Home Run Inn, etc. Thus, you should have some type of food to let the volunteers know that you appreciate them.

## VIII.  SOCIAL MEDIA

Design a social media plan which includes the board members. We are all familiar with Facebook, LinkedIn, Twitter, Instagram, and many other social media sites that will be part of the PR and marketing side of the NFP organization.

Setup each page consistently across the board, so that when someone sees the name of the NFP, logo, and photos that they know it is pertaining to the organization. Connect as many of them as possible so whatever you put on one, the post will appear on the other. Keep it professional because the NFP is a business.

Have each board member voluntarily put something together pertaining to their area of practice of the NFP to post on the social media sites. This will keep them involved in the social media side of the NFP. Let the board know that it is about the NFP and not individuals. Therefore, each board member should be able to sign in where the logo or name appears on every post.

Create **signup here** and **fill-in** forms to gather information so that people can be added to the mailing list. Offer a free booklet or something in return that is cost efficient. Keep everyone that signed up informed of events and progress of the NFP through social media and newsletters. Find ways to present the NFP as a social site where the general public can depend on receiving valuable and helpful information that pertains to the NFP.

Design secured **DONATE** here buttons making it easy for Donors and contributors to make donations. Be sure that an automatic response will appear thanking Donors for their contributions. Make donating as seamlessly as possible.

## IX.    CROWD FUNDING

What is Crowd Funding? Now, we will look at what is called Crowd Funding.  In Crowd Funding, you would develop a campaign that is online, and some are attach to the NFPs social media that you have setup. The purpose is to encourage people to support your cause. You can receive funding from the range of book publication, playwriting, and movie development. It is endless to what people will support.

A list of popular crowd funding sites is listed below.  Some are free while others charge a percentage or a flat fee.  They all have terms of agreement so read through carefully before deciding.  Some will just give you the information, and you must do everything else yourself, while others will setup, monitor, and supervise your site:

- Seed Chicago (Google search)
- Small Business Improvement Fund (SBIF) (https://www.cityofchicago.org/city/en/depts/dcd/supp_info/small_business_improvementfundsbif.html)
- Accion Chicago (https://accionchicago.org/)
- Indiegogo (https://www.indiegogo.com/en)
- Kickstarter (https://www.kickstarter.com/)
- GoFundMe (https://www.gofundme.com/)
- Angel Investment Group (http://www.invstor.com/information/angel-investors/angel-investor-group)
- truCrowd (https://us.trucrowd.com/)
- Fundageek (http://fundageek.net/)
- RocketHub (https://www.rockethub.com/)
- Equity (http://www.equity.net/)

For those who are running a NFP in other states, look for funding in that state.

## X.  BANKS

Make a list of banks starting with your own and the board members and their CRA Officers/Vice Presidents for Monetary Donations and seek out REO Officers regarding donations of properties.

1.  ______________________________________________

2.  ______________________________________________

3.  ______________________________________________

4.  ______________________________________________

5.  ______________________________________________

6.  ______________________________________________

7.  ______________________________________________

8.  ______________________________________________

9.  ______________________________________________

10  ______________________________________________


List Companies that are Going Out of Business that can Assist Your NFP

1.  ______________________________________
2.  ______________________________________
3.  ______________________________________
4.  ______________________________________
5.  ______________________________________
6.  ______________________________________
7.  ______________________________________
8.  ______________________________________
9.  ______________________________________
10. ______________________________________

List Schools that are Closing:

1.  ______________________________________
2.  ______________________________________

3. _______________________________________

4. _______________________________________

5. _______________________________________

6. _______________________________________

7. _______________________________________

8. _______________________________________

9. _______________________________________

10. ______________________________________

## Collaborations

List three (3) NFPs that have a similar mission as your organization:

1. _______________________________________

2. _______________________________________

3. _______________________________________

List three (3) NFPs whose mission differ from your organization, yet they can benefit your organization

1. _______________________________________

2. _______________________________________

3. _______________________________________

## Networking

List three (3) associations that your staff and board members can attend networking events:

1. _______________________________________

2. _______________________________________

3. _______________________________________

## Professional Associations

List three (3) NFPs professional associations that you can attend meetings to stay current on shifts and changing trends of NFPs.

1. _______________________________________

2. _______________________________________

3. _______________________________________

## **Established Not-for-Profit**

List three well known NFPs in your area with similar mission and goals that you can shadow and ask pertinent questions regarding how to serve.

1. ______________________________________________

2. ______________________________________________

3. ______________________________________________

# DIVISION III - Grant Writing Formats

We will cover in this section: Grants, Different Types of Grants, Letter of Intent/Letter of Inquiry, Standard Business/Grant Proposal, Grant Research, and Links to Funders.

## I. WHAT IS A GRANT?

A grant is free money.  You do not have to pay back.  If someone tells you that you must pay back money, then it is not a grant.  NFPs can apply for grants from foundations, corporations, and local/federal government entities.

How do grants come about?  As a citizen, you pay taxes to the city, the state, the county, and the federal government. A portion goes toward paying public workers, rendering services, and grants issued to organizations and/or companies to provide those services.

Another way that grant monies is formulated is through businesses that have promised to give back to the communities that have patronized them.  The businesses create foundations with profits that are distributed to NFPs in the form of grants.  This is done in exchange to receiving tax breaks from the government. Then you have family foundations set up where family members govern over monies that was generated or inherited and they issue grants to NFPs.  Now, here is the key, NFPs with the 501c3 determination status from the Internal Revenue Service can receive grants. To receive a grant, some form of "Grant Writing" often referred to as either a proposal or an application is usually required.

Most grants are made to fund a specific project and require some level of compliance and reporting. The grant writing process involves an applicant submitting a proposal (or submission) to a potential funder, either on the applicant's own initiative or in response to a <u>Request for Proposal</u> from the funder. Other grants can be given to individuals, such as victims of natural disasters or individuals who seek to open a small business. Sometimes grant makers require grant seekers to have some form of tax-exempt status registered as a nonprofit organization or a local government.

For example, tiered funding for a freeway are very large grants negotiated at a government agency (e.g., municipal government). Project-related funding involving governments, businesses, communities, and individuals is often arranged by application either in writing or online.

1. What is a grant? _________________________________________

_________________________________________________________

_________________________________________________________

2. How are grants created? __________________________________

_________________________________________________________

_________________________________________________________

_________________________________________________________

_________________________________________________________

3. What is an alternative name for a grant? ___________________

_________________________________________________________

_________________________________________________________

4. Can individuals obtain grants? ____________________________

## II.  DIFFERENT TYPES OF GRANTS

Different types of grants are: (1) business grants; (2) educational grants; (3) technology grants; (4) medical grants; (5) construction grants; (6) corporate grants; and (7) more. Whatever grant you are applying for, be sure it is in line with the NFP organization that you oversee.

In our local government there are 12 cabinets. Each cabinet represents the public service industry in which you can apply for grants. For example, The Department of Transportation, the Department of

Education, the Department of Agricultural, the Department of Commerce, etc.

## III.    LETTER OF INTENT?

There are two most common ways to attain grant money.  The first way to get money is to write a Letter of Intent ("LI") a/k/a Letter of Inquiry ("LQ"). The second is to write a standard business grant proposal which will be discussed next. Most Funders would like to see the LI first and then when they become interested, they would want a standard business grant proposal submitted. A LI for a grant is designed to generate interest from a grant provider. It indicates core activities and projects of the organization applying for the grant. The letter can serve as a request for funding or materials to submit a full grant. A grant must be written and signed by the organization's director or operations coordinator. This request for application materials also includes information on when you intend to apply for the grant.

1.   What is a Letter of Intent?

____________________________________________________

____________________________________________________

2.   Why should a Letter of Intent be submitted instead of a grant proposal? ___________________________________________

____________________________________________________

____________________________________________________

____________________________________________________

The LI is really a mini proposal. The LI is a one-page document and should be typed on a font size of eleven (11). You must have the ability to get to the point and briefly state the reason for the grant.  You must be concise.  Some Funders are too busy to read a full proposal and will gladly read a LI which has eight (8) parts to it.  The following makes up the LI format:

- Heading
- Address
- Regarding
- Salutation/Greeting
- Introduction

- Body
- Closing
- Signature Block

Let's cover each part that makes up the LI. The date should be when the letter(s) is going to be mailed and not the date that it is typed. Below are the different parts of the LI:

## Heading

First you need your organization's stationery. The stationery should have at the very top the name of the NFP organization, location, phone number, fax number (optional), website, and email address.

## ADDRESS

Prior to sending off the LI, you need to contact the Funders and ask who should the letter be addressed. Upon obtaining that information also acquire about the person's job title. You may be told that a certain committee, board, or even a marketing department handles the LI/LQ.

Job Title - The job title of the individual should be listed under their name.

Company Name - You will type the company's full name including abbreviations and or symbols.

Location - Make sure you have the exact address, suite number, mail code, and the right building. A lot of Funders have more than one building. Find out if there is a corporate office to send the LI/LQ.

## REGARDING

The regard is the actual intentions or purpose of the letter. See example below

### Re: *Letter of Intent - General Operation Support*

The above is an example of how to type the purpose of a letter. The most common Re lines are general operation support, seed money a/k/a startup, program development, or capital campaign. There are many others.

## SALUTATION/GREETING

The greeting can be addressed to an individual, board, committee, public relation, marketing department, communication, etc. You should start with Dear Mr. or Ms. [last name].

## INTRODUCTION

The introduction is after the greeting and is the first paragraph of the LI, and should include in your writing the following:

- Credentials of organization
- Service history
- Location

Think of the LI as a business card. You are introducing the organization to the Funders. In the first paragraph, you should begin with the name of the organization, your 501c3 status, how long the NFP been established and what community or township (*i.e.*, East-Garfield) is the organization located, the side of town (westside). You need to let Funders know that the NFP is inner city or rural as well. Inform them, what city, state, and county that the NFP resides. Next provide the services that are provided by the NFP and an overall description that will sum up the staff and volunteers in terms of education and experience.

## BODY OF LETTER

You want to identify your target population which are the people that you provide services. How do you describe the target population? You may state their gender male, female, transgender, lesbian, gay, bisexual, and queer, and economics if they are low income, middle class, recipient of governmental benefits such as social security or public aide benefits.

You can describe them socially as disadvantaged, homeless, substance abusers, victim of domestic violence, juvenile delinquent, HIV, LGBTGIA, men, women and children, seniors, or youth.

Describe clients' positions in society of their educational background, high school drop-outs, elementary students, secondary students, etc. It is within the body of the letter that you are telling the funder what it is that you now want to do and why funding is being sought.

Answer the following questions in the LI: (1) Do you want to expand the NFP services? (2) Do you want to hire more program staff? (3) Do you want to update equipment? This is the time to sell yourself.

You can describe their ethnicity. Are they African-American, European, Hispanic, or Asian. Are you providing services for cross cultures? Multi-cultural? Diverse? When it comes to age, you may give an age range which your services cover 14 to 18, 55 and up, etc. or just classify them as youth, adults, or seniors.

## CLOSING

In the third paragraph which is where you conclude the letter and sum up and summarize your request which reflects the regard part of the letter. You then give contact information of you or a designated person.

## SIGNATURE BLOCK

This is where you end the letter with Sincerely, Cordially, or whatever term is appropriate. Leave four (4) spaces and type your name and job title.

On the next page, there is an example of a LI provided from Safe Haven Community Center to National City Bank. This letter is not *written in stone* and can be written to fit your NFP. This letter was funded.

*Safe Haven Community Skill Center*
*3243 W. Warren #101*
*Chicago, Illinois 60624*
*773-426-0271*
*eurydicemoore@yahoo.com*
*www.1010skillcenter.com*

*May 15, 2006*

*Ms. Cassandra Slade*
*CRA Officer*
*National City Bank*
*1 North Franklin*
*25th Floor*
*Chicago, Illinois 60606*

*Re:  Letter of Intent Financial Literacy Education Conference*

*Dear Ms. Slade,*

*The Safe Haven Community Skill Center is a non-for-profit charitable 501c3 organization located in the East-Garfield Community on the west side of Chicago. We have provided alternative educational services for low to moderate income disadvantage individuals that have been unemployed, or underemployed, and those that are seeking career mobility or advancement.  In addition, we have provided workshops, seminars, and job trainings for service providers from the field of education, social services, community development, and faith base.*

*Our Instructional and Programmatic services are delivered in a workshop, or seminar format.  The job trainings have been in proposal writing, case management, non-profit management, faith base counseling, and financial literacy education.  We propose to host a city-wide financial literacy conference for 100 social service, educational, community development, and faith base providers on Sunday September 10, 2006 at the Chicago Marriott located in the Medical District Area from 2:00 p.m. to 5:00 p.m. to conclude with a wrap up focus group and dinner.*

*The goal of the conference is to equip service providers with tools for empowerment for the purpose to better serve their communities.  The conference will host four presenters in proposal writing, credit repair, and debt reduction, financial banking services, and local resource information.  Upon completion of each workshop service, providers will receive certificates to validate and certify their attendance and continuing educational training.  Each service provider will receive workshop materials, resources, educational gifts, and door prizes.*

*The requested funding for this program is $1,500.  If you need further information, please contact me at (773) 426-0271.*

*Sincerely,*

*Eurydice Moore, M.A. Ph.D.*
*Chief Executive Officer/Educator*

What are the eight parts of the LI?

A. _______________________________

B. _______________________________

C. _______________________________

D. _______________________________

E. _______________________________

F. _______________________________

G. _______________________________

H. _______________________________


Use the information below to start creating the LI for your NFP:

<u>Write your organization's general information below</u>:

A.  Organization's Name
B.  Organization's Address
C.  Organization's telephone number
D.  Organization's Website
E.  Organization's Email Address
F.  Any other pertinent information

_______________________________

_______________________________

_______________________________

_______________________________

_______________________________

_______________________________

_______________________________

<u>Select a target date which you would like to submit letters</u>:

(_________ ___, 20___)

<u>Select a funder for the salutation and list the following information</u>:

A.  Funder Contact person's name _______________________

B.  Job title _______________________________________

C.  Address_________________________________________

D.  City, State Zip Code_______________________________

List why you are contacting them in the 'Re:' section of the LETTER.

<u>Select only one item from below</u>:

    A.  General Operation Support
    B.  Program Development
    C.  Startup
    D.  Capital Campaign

<u>Select from below the appropriate greeting for the funder contact person(s)</u>:

    Selection: _________________

    A.  Mr.
    B.  Mrs.
    C.  Ms.
    D.  Dr.
    E.  Attorney "Esq."
    F.  Congressman
    G.  State Representative
    H.  State Senator
    I.  To Whom It May Concern
    J.  Board of Directors
    K.  Board Members
    L.  Marketing Department
    M.  Donation Committee
    N.  Appropriation Committee

<u>Select the credentials to be used in your introduction section of your letter</u>:

***The organization is a***

- 501(c)(3) Exempt Organization;
- 501(c)(3) Not-for-Profit; or
- 501(c)(3) Organization.

***The organization has been in existence***

List the number of years or give the articles of incorporation month, day, and year.

***List the history of the organization***

Write the mission statement of the organization.

<u>Program Services</u>:

> List and describe the target population which your organization provide program services for children, youth, women, men, seniors, homeless, and/or low-income.

<u>Staff Background</u>:

> Education and/or experience in providing services.

<u>Identify and select the reason for writing the funder, this is the body of the letter by answering the following questions</u>:

> Want to expand program?
>
> Want to update equipment?
>
> Want to hire more people?
>
> General operation support?
>
> Program development?
>
> Want to renovate?
>
> Want to include additional communities?
>
> Want to add more target populations?

Please include in your writing the Who? What? When? Where? and How?

This section of the LI requires your closing in which you summarize the purpose of the letter whether monetary or nonmonetary below is some examples for you to choose:

- We are requesting $36,000 for general operation support of our organization,
- We are requesting 30 computers for installation into our new computer lab,
- We are requesting office furniture to furnish our three offices which will consist of desks and chairs, and
- We are requesting $25,000 to cover the cost of training materials for 20 new program recruits.

The ending of the letter would conclude with:

A. Determine who will be your organization contact person,
B. Contact person telephone number,
C. Request for additional information,
D. Thank you for reviewing the letter,
E. Ending letter with sincerely, best regards, or regards,
F. Name of person who wrote letter in printed form,
G. Name of person who wrote letter in a signature, and
H. Job title of person who wrote letter.

The second way to get money is to apply for grants. Grants may vary based on the organization or agency providing it. Be sure to follow their guidelines with the content that you are about to learn. Grants can be in the format of an online application, hardcopy, grant application, narrative, federal and state. It is important to be aware of the eligibility requirements, guidelines, and timely submission of the grant. Below we will discuss what is known as a standard grant a/k/a narrative or generic grant.

## IV.  STANDARD BUSINESS/GRANT PROPOSAL

What is a standard grant? A standard grant has the fundamental components of a grant yet is not based on any Funder specific guidelines. You are not putting a grant together based on instructions from the Funder. Below are the components of a standard grant proposal and checklist to use when formatting the Standard Business/Grant Proposal:

- Mission Statement

- History
- Grant Request
- Need Statement
- Program Description
- Methodology
- Goals
- Objectives
- Evaluation
- Collaboration
- Sustainability
- Letter of Support
- Supporting Documents

Mission Statement:

The mission statement is the purpose that your organization was formed.  It also consists of the organization's beliefs and philosophy. The mission statement is usually one to two sentences that entails the purpose, philosophy and belief of the organization. You can refer to your organization's document a/k/a Articles of Incorporation.  See Division I NFP Setup.

1.  What is the fundamental component parts of a grant?

_______________________________________________________________
_______________________________________________________________
_______________________________________________________________
_______________________________________________________________

2.  What is a mission statement?

_______________________________________________________________
_______________________________________________________________
_______________________________________________________________
_______________________________________________________________

History:

You can refer to the LI, which is really a mini proposal. In this section, write about your organization, and add your organization's uniqueness. You should also mention approximately two to three organizations that are addressing the same community issues that you are seeking funding and describe what will set your organization apart. Next describe why you should be given the opportunity to throw your hat into the ring, and what you would do differently from other organizations.

Grant Request:

In this section, give a lump sum monetary request (*i.e.*, We are seeking funding in the amount of $XXX,XXX for general operation support, which will cover rental, utilities, and program services.).

Need Statement:

In this section, describe the community problem(s), it is advised to select one to three issues to write about in the proposal, and describe how the organization plan to address those issues. It is in this section that you present the most recent statistical data to back up your findings and observations. You may use the following sources to assist you in that endeavor:

- US Censor,
- Police Department,
- Educational Resources,
- Journals,
- Internet Searches,
- City Departments,
- Newspaper clippings, watch dog group surveys and reports,
- Focus Group, and
- Quotes from Leading Experts.

Program Description:

In this section, describe the What? Who? When? Where? Why? and How? What is the program that you are seeking funding? Describe the target population that the program services are designated. Give the timeline of the program. Give the date that the program is going to start. Is this a one-time program? Is this program seasonal? Is this a perpetual program? Is this program temporary? If any programs are seasonal or temporary, then give the start and ending date of the program services. Provide the funder with the location of the program. The funder(s) should be made aware if it's going to be on-site or off-site (the location of your non-profit or another location).  If the program is not at the NFP, then where exactly?  If the program is on the first floor? Basement? Room 411? Green room? then indicate the exact place.

Funders also want to know why you are doing this program.  What need are you hoping to address and what is the expected end? Will providing this service expand and increase or decrease and eradicate? (Example, if you are addressing teen pregnancies and notice that the community has a high rate, indicate the purpose of the program.) Let's say 10% of the neighborhood girls are coming up pregnant.  You want to introduce a program to offer alternatives to premarital sex.  You hope to reduce teen pregnancies by 5%.

Lastly, you want to describe the how this program is going to operate also known as the methodology.  You are going to describe the day and hours of operation, and when the program starts and end or is perpetual. Then list the activities. Include a list of job titles and descriptions of those involved with the program as well as whether they are staff or volunteers.  You will describe this program from conception to delivery.  It would also be beneficial to provide a timeline in the form of a diagram or chart to give Donors a visual view.

An example of a Methodology is below:

| Tasks | Personnel | Deadline |
|---|---|---|
| Planning Stage | Executive Director and Team | 02/01/2017 |
| Section of Site | Executive Director and Team | 03/15/2017 |
| Selection of Staff | Executive Director and Team | 05/01/2017 |

Goal:

A goal is a general statement. It is defined as the result or achievement toward which effort is directed or aimed. A terminal point. (Example, to feed people, to assist people in living a better lifestyle, to help homeless people find housing, etc.)

Objectives:

Objectives are specific, detailed and measurable. The activities that will help you accomplish your goals, will lead you to accomplishing your organization's mission. Notice the difference between the example of goal and objective. Once again, a goal is a general statement. There is no way you can prove you fed people. The objective gives you activities that can be documented and proven.

Objective Example:

To distribute food to 500 African-American males and females from low to moderate income households from 18 to 65 years of age from the East-Garfield Community.

Evaluation:

You must have an evaluation component within your proposal in which you can determine that the mission, goal, and objective of the proposal was met. Below are a few evaluation tools to assist in the determination if the mission, goal, and the objective of the organization was met:

- Application
- Sign-in sheet
- Pre and Post test
- Survey
- Questionnaires
- Testimony
- Interview
- Consultant
- Skill assessment - rating system
- Other

Collaboration:

A lot of proposals are now requiring team efforts among organizations and usually a lead organization will be designated. Funders have now become cost effective. If you are part of a collaborative effort, make sure you know the organization and that your organization's name is listed in the proposal as well. It is also for your information that you should put together either a Linkage Agreement or Memorandum of Understanding. It is amazing that when funding comes in, people tend to forget. Whether you use a Linkage Agreement or a Memorandum of Understanding it should have the names of all organizations that is to be involved with the project and what each will bring to the table, and then the Executive Directors or designated representative(s) should sign off on the document and obtain a copy.

Sustainable:

Funding usually last a calendar year. In some cases, you are invited to resubmit proposals. There are Funders that fund projects two, three, or five calendar years. Some Funders will inform you that it's a onetime deal. Whatever the case may be, if Funders cease to provide funding, your organization will be able to continue providing services and not have to close shop. Funders are now beginning to request a sustainability plan as a component of the proposal. How do you plan to continue supporting your non-profit?

Below are examples of sustainability plans:

Letter of Support:

Some Funders will require especially the state and federal grants for you to submit a Letter of Support. This letter is from an alderman or congressman, usually a governmental official or leading authority familiar with the organization and can vouch for you. The submission of this document is very impressive.

Supporting Documents:

Once the proposal is completed there are attachments that need to be submitted along with the proposal and they are listed below:

- Articles of Incorporation
- Board List
- Bylaws
- Insurance*
- Financial Statement
- Bond*
- Linkage Agreement/Memorandum of Understanding

- Resumes
- Job Descriptions
- Copy of Statistical Data
- Brochure
- Newspaper Clipping on Organization
- Website
- Email (Note: Not all Funders requires)*
- Audit*

* Depending on the Funder, you may not need to provide these documents.

The following Standard Grant Proposal was funded and is used in this booklet as an example:

---

**STANDARD BUSINESS PROPOSAL**

Eurydice
3600 N. Halsted
Chicago, Illinois
773-544-5341

Business Start-Up

**Mission Statement:**

The mission of Eurydice is to develop leaders by taking the complexity of business and simplify it through training and development, one-on-one, group sessions through business coaching. Eurydice will assist individuals who want to setup a Non-Profit through Incorporation and 501c3. In addition, Eurydice will offer Training and Development, along with Boot Camps. Eurydice will also assist clients in the development of business start-up and ventures which will generate revenues to assist Non-Profits in sustainability and organizational independence. The targeted population will be ministers, college students, teachers, and emerging Non-Profit leaders.

**History:**

The Owner of Eurydice have 30 years of combined education and experience in Human Services Administration, Not-for-Profit Consultation and Management, advance certificate in teaching entrepreneurship education, and a business startup certificate from City Colleges of Chicago and City of Chicago's Department of Business Affairs.

---

**Grant Request:**

We are requesting a grant of $10,906 in startup for business training courses and publishing of books for business services.

**Need for Services:**

According to the United States market research report June 2015, the business coach industry is a $12 billion industry which is expected to increase in the next five years, and thereafter experience continued growth due to increasing competition among corporations, globalization, and the emerging of domestic competitors will encourage companies to spend in this industry, along with the widespread use of technology and an aging work force demand for services provided by this industry. According to the Donor Forum of Illinois there are more than 1.5 million Non-Profits in the United States.

The State of Illinois comprise data that the employment trend is one out of every nine private jobs is in the Non-Profit sector, and have been growing in the recent years due to the economy, crime, and sociological issues. Due to the rapid change in technology, governmental cut backs, and decline in donations, business coaches are in demand to assist organizations in training and development, strategic planning and sustainability action plans for the continual survival of Non-Profits. Business coaches are also in demand to assist Non-Profits in accomplishing their missions.

Therefore, the target market will be ministers, teachers, college students, and emerging Non-Profit leaders. The target market will be 30-50 years of age, single/married, urban residents, males and females, multicultural ethnicity with an economic base between $30,000 and $60,000.

The target market place will be churches, schools, and colleges. Staff will conduct outreach searches for target markets through daily calls, onsite presentations, word of mouth, referrals, and advertisements to alert for available services.

Colleges and universities strength are that they offer degree programs and have professors that are in the industry. However, due to governmental cut backs in financial aides and student loan debts, enrollment has declined. Students are seeking other options to acquire the skills needed for their career goals and missions.

In addition, the growth rate for private colleges and universities is 1.7, the growth rate of community colleges is -0.4, and For-Profit universities is -0.1, including costly tuition.

Eurydice offers affordable prices lower than competitors yet compromising quality services and have continued ongoing contact with clients after completion of services through business coaching via conference calls, consultations, hotlines, and weekly mentoring.

**Services:**

Eurydice is providing the following services to current and new residents:

- Consultation
- Non-Church 501c3
- Training and Development
- Non-Profit Boot Camp
- For-Profit Boot Camp

**Goal and Objectives:**

The goal of Eurydice is to assist clients in business startup.

1. To recruit 12 Clients,

2. To conduct 12 Consultations,

3. To complete 12 IRS 501c3 Determinations,

3. To provide four Training and Development Sessions,

4. To provide two Non-Profit Boot Camps, and

5. To provide two For-Profit Boot Camps.

**Methodology:**

Eurydice will be an appointment only home-base and mobile operation. The business operates Monday through Saturday from 9:00 a.m. to 6:00 p.m. The business is a For-Profit located in the Lakeview community on the north side of Chicago, Illinois. Clients will complete a client registration form and a questionnaire. Staff will provide a consultation in which an interview and an assessment will be conducted to identify the services needed. Clients will be assisted in the incorporation and 501c3 process. Clients will be enrolled based on recommendation into appropriate training and development in both Non-Profit and For-Profit boot camps. Training and boot camps will cover set ups, operation, policies, management, and the development of a sustainability plan. Each client will be eligible for the business coaching which will consist of conference calls, hotlines, mentoring, strategic planning and leadership development. A curriculum in a text book format will be issued. The curriculum is unique that it is flexible, and clients can work at their own pace. Material will be provided explaining step-by-step; therefore, assisting clients in identifying goals, objectives, and action plans.

**Marketing:**

Eurydice marketing goals for the businesses are to implement primary market strategies of direct/outside sale calls, clients' incentive referral program, brand promotional activities, and advertising to grow the business. In addition, the business will strive to add one new client a month.

Our secondary marketing strategies will consist of the following and will be administered accordingly:

Direct/outside calls
Direct mail
Word of mouth
Display advertising/print ads
Tradeshows/conventions/fairs
Yellow pages
Networking
Publicity
Promotional Activities
Website
Blogging
Emails

**Business Startup Budget**

| | |
|---|---|
| 6 Weeks Business Coaching & Mentoring Curriculum | $3,950 |
| Book Publishing | $6,956 |
| | **$10,906** |

**Evaluation:**

The goals and objectives will be measured through program participants enrollment, attendance records, questionnaires, and copies of IRS 501c3 determination letters. We will also have a consultant to observe and complete a report of programs, and fiscal operations.

In Summary:

Grant writing although tedious is yet very interesting. I have shared the fundamentals which disclose the two most common formats of any grant. You now have the tools to understand and write an actual grant from scratch. Grants can take the form of an application, online applying, two to five sheets to over 100 pages. Whatever the case may be or the format, there are key elements across the board. You learn the fundamentals. It doesn't matter the format of a grant. The key to submission is to give whatever is requested no more and no less.

Lastly, you want to keep a tracking system for all LIs and grant proposals sent out. The date of submission, the funder's name, and a follow up section along with information if Funders were contacted about anything and if proposal was accepted or denied.

Now that you have viewed how to write both a LI and a Standard Grant Proposal, it is time to research. A list of websites to visit to research grant information has been provided in this booklet. Once you begin your search for Funders to save time, seek out those with similar missions and make sure you are in their geographic areas, and meet their eligibility requirements. Some Funders may provide contact information in which you can contact them directly.

The Standard Business/Grant Proposal is not the only way to apply for grants. You can log on and fill out grant applications to foundations, banks, companies, and city/state/federal. Be prepared to spend as much time as needed to fill-out the application because some will not allow you to save or print.

Below are Grant research resources to get you started on your journey:

- Guide Star
- The grantsmanship center
- The council on foundation
- Foundationsearch.com
- Fundsnetservices.com
- The Chronicle of Philanthropy

- Grants.gov
- Forefront.com
- Grant Station
- Tech Soup
- The grants funding network
- Novartis Patient Assistance Foundation, Inc.
- Wells Fargo Foundation
- The Walmart Foundation, Inc.
- The Bank of America Charitable Foundation, Inc.
- The JP Morgan Chase Foundation
- The Target Foundation

## V.   GRANT RESEARCH - HOW TO DETERMINE A GRANT REQUEST

1. Research the cost to operate your organization,
2. Create a budget for your organization, and
3. Have a budget for each program services.

Once you can determine the dollar amount required, you will know the monetary funding amount needed.

Please see the organizational budget in Division I of the NFP section of this book. This will give you an idea of what to include in your budget.

1. List the name of the community(ies) that the NFP serve:

    ______________________________

    ______________________________

    ______________________________

    ______________________________

    ______________________________

    ______________________________

    ______________________________

2.  List the boundaries N, S, E, and W of the community(ies) where the NFP is located:

    ______________________________

    ______________________________

_______________________________

_______________________________

_______________________________

_______________________________

_______________________________

3.  List three issues within that community(ies):

_________________________________________________

_________________________________________________

_________________________________________________

4.  Identify one issue to focus on in the grant: _____________________

_________________________________________________

_________________________________________________

5.  Research and assemble statistics regarding the issue for use. What are the statistics? _______________________________________

_________________________________________________

_________________________________________________

6.  Review Division III need statement section and select statistical data. _______________________________________________

_________________________________________________

_________________________________________________

7.  List three other NFPs within the community:

_________________________________________________

_________________________________________________

_________________________________________________

8.  Review their program services.
9.  How are your NFP's program like theirs?
10. How does your NFP's program differ from theirs?
11. What is your uniqueness?
12. What is the program services that you intend to offer to address the issue(s) within the community(ies)?
13. Will you have other NFPs as collaborators?  If so, Identify them.  If you plan to have others you must prior to including them into the proposal have met with them and have completed a Memorandum of Understanding.

## VI.  LINKS TO GRANT FUNDING

The following links are a benefit to you in order to have access to an array of options that will assist you in seeking funding for your NFP organization.

http://giving.walmart.com/foundation

https://www.insidephilanthropy.com/grants-for-k-12-education/macys-inc-grants-for-k-12-education.html

https://www.insidephilanthropy.com/grants-for-k-12-education/the-coca-cola-foundation-grants-for-k-12-education.html

http://elizabethtayloraidsfoundation.org/

https://corporate.homedepot.com/community/home-depot-foundation-grants

https://newscenter.dollargeneral.com/our-story/blog-posts/dollar-general-literacy-foundation-grant-applications-now-open.htm

https://corporate.target.com/corporate-responsibility/grants/target-foundation-grants

https://www.unitedwayoc.org/community-partners/grant-making/?gclid=EAIaIQobChMIxeytoo7O1QIVESlpCh3AsQD3EAAYASAAEgL8vfD_BwE

http://www.goodsports.org/?gclid=EAIaIQobChMIvOrj0I7O1QIVxbfACh2WUAuTEAAYAiAAEgLehPD_BwE

http://ysa.org/grants/

http://youth.gov/funding-search/federal-youth-funding-agencies

https://about.bankofamerica.com/en-us/what-guides-us/find-grants-sponsorships.html#fbid=Bt3phRkSlyX

http://www.polkbrosfdn.org/

http://www.earts.org/grants?gclid=EAIaIQobChMI1_7cjJDO1QIV0LrACh25qwg3EAAYASAAEgKoN_D_BwE

https://www.cityofchicago.org/city/en/depts/dca/provdrs/grants.html

http://www.arts.illinois.gov/grants-programs

https://www.macfound.org/

https://www.tgci.com/funding-sources/Funders/panera-bread-foundation-inc

https://www.mccormickfoundation.org/

http://illinoisjumpstart.org/scholarships-grants/

https://www.bcbsil.com/company-info/community-involvement/grant-sponsorship

https://sparkplugfoundation.org/

http://www.honda.com/about?id=ahf

http://safewayfoundation.org/get-funded/what-we-fund.html

http://www.grantsforteachers.com/corporate-grants/lockheed_martin_corporation_grants/grantdetails_61.aspx

https://www.wishyouwellfoundation.org/apply/

http://www.awesomefoundation.org/en/faq

http://www.childrensobesityfund.org/grantfundraising-faq/

http://www.rgkfoundation.org/#programs

https://www.toyota.com/usa/community/articles/community_grants_foundation.html

http://www.fordfoundation.org/work/our-grants/

https://www.sony.com/en_us/SCA/social-responsibility/giving-guidelines.html

https://www.tdbank.com/net/selectstate.aspx?ref=/community/charitable_foundation_grant.html

http://www.shell.us/sustainability/request-for-a-grant-from-shell.html

http://www.halliburton.com/en-US/about-us/community/halliburton-foundation/default.page?node-id=hgeyxt9a

https://online.foundationsource.com/andrew/juniorboard2.htm

http://dudleytdoughertyfoundation.org/submit_grant

https://www.doleliving.com/grants/national-art-education-foundation

https://www.americanimmigrationcouncil.org/community-grants

http://www.mazdafoundation.org/grant-guidelines/

http://tarrantfoundation.org/

https://www.pnc.com/en/about-pnc/corporate-responsibility/philanthropy/pnc-foundation.html

http://lanlfoundation.org/education-community-grants

https://www.ed.gov/category/subject/Grants

http://www.gofreegovernmentmoney.com/grants_for_business?ref=bingads-grants&utm_source=bing&utm_medium=cpc&utm_campaign=Free%20Grants%20Community&utm_term=grants&utm_content=grants

http://peoplesgasdelivery.com/company/involvement.aspx

http://toolboxforeducation.com/

https://naaee.org/eepro/opportunities/disney-summer-service-grants

http://www.businesswire.com/news/home/20140218006383/en/Jo-Ann-Gave-29-Million-Non-Profit-Organizations-Fiscal

https://www.google.com/search?q=ray+charles+foundation+general+grants&oq=ray+charles+foundation+general+grants&aqs=chrome..69i57.16280j0j4&sourceid=chrome&ie=UTF-8

# RESOURCE DEVELOPMENT
## GOING TO THE NEXT LEVEL

http://www.newschools.org/invent/

http://hjweinbergfoundation.org/grants/

http://www.ppgcommunities.com/Home.aspx

http://www.benefits.va.gov/gibill/education_programs.asp

https://www.thecne.org/engage/grants/

https://www.statefarm.com/about-us/community/education-programs/grants-scholarships/company-grants

https://www.neafoundation.org/pages/resources-other-grant-opportunities

http://www.aauw.org/what-we-do/educational-funding-and-awards/community-action-grants/

https://corporate.bestbuy.com/community-grants-page/

https://bobwoodrufffoundation.org/?gclid=EAIaIQobChMI5pu-yezP1QIVjzVpCh0LrQkCEAMYAyAAEgIR_vD_BwE

https://www.charleskochfoundation.org/apply-for-grants/requests-proposals/?gclid=EAIaIQobChMI5pu-yezP1QIVjzVpCh0LrQkCEAMYASAAEgLLLvD_BwE

http://www.ppgcommunities.com/Our-Story/Education.aspx

https://brooksbrotherscorporate.requestitem.com/

## Additional Acknowledgements

I would like to as always acknowledge God my Creator who has guided me through this life of service.

I would like to acknowledge my daughter Rita McClendon, who has been an eye witness of accounts of many trials and triumphs that I have experienced. She has always been by my side.

I would like to acknowledge Patricia Barto who passed many years ago. Oh, how I long for her. Patricia connected me to the opportunity to work in a hospital laboratory and en route to become a Medical Laboratory Technician with the designated ASCP recognition in the field of Medical Laboratory Technology.

I will always acknowledge Anna White & Annie Norwood my maternal great-grandmother and grandmother who were very instrumental in my life. My great-grand mother is the person that I acquired organizational skills, the love of travel, and the spirit of an entrepreneurship. Annie my grandmother was instrumental in encouraging me to pursue opportunities. She had a discerning eye. It's because of her that I learned to drive, type, participated in a cotillion, and entered the ministry.

# Dr. Eurydice Moore, Business Consultant

## Founder of Eurydice

- Assisted Churches, Schools, and Agencies in acquiring over 3 Million in Resource Development Funding
- An Author of 4 books: Riddy Ann against the ODD, how to set up a Not-for-Profit, A-Z guide in for profit set up, Resource Development a New level of Dimension
- Grew up in Chicago's East-Garfield Community & graduated from Lucy Flower H.S.1974
- Graduated from Central YMCA in A.S degree in Medical Laboratory Technology 1976
- Graduated from College of St. Francis in B.S. degree in Health Arts 1984
- Graduated from Spertus in M.S. in Human Services Administration 1986
- Graduated from Concordia University in M.A. in Urban Education 1993
- Graduated from Northern Illinois's in Advance Certificate in Entrepreneurship Program 1991
- Graduated from Midwest Theological Institute in Indiana in Ph.D. Pastoral Counseling 2004
- Completed City of Chicago's Business Affairs & City College Business Start up 2007
- Completed Mormans Consulting Group's Business Coaching & Business Strategies Trainings 2016
- Medical Laboratory Technician at Rush, Cook County, Mount Sinai, Mary Thompson University of Illinois of Chicago Hospitals 1973-1985
- Educator & Work Study Coordinator at Lucy Flower H.S. 1985-1991
- Guidance Counselor at Morton Career Academy 1991-1995
- Over 30 years of combine Non-for-Profit experiences at Chicago Public School System, Churches, Social Services Center, Safe Haven Community Skill Center & Hannah Community Development Center 1985-2004
- Established Eurydice Moore & Associates 2004 to presence served over 12,000 clients in distribution of free grant and resource development information, incorporation, and 501(c)(3)
- Established Eurydice January 2016 to offer business set up, coaching,

trainings & development, incorporation, 501(c)(3) set up, grant writing, and resource development.
- Internet & Radio Personality 2005-2007
- CAN TV program in Non-Profit & For-Profit Business Resource 2007-2009

Author's Contact Information:

Dr. Eurydice Moore
eurydicemoore1@gmail

Discounted books are available to those who are interested in teaching from this booklet. You may contact me at the above-mentioned email address for discounted books, Consultation Services, Training and Development, and/or Speaking Engagements.

To add to your arsenal, PURCHASE MY BOOK "For-Profit Business" in order to add additional information. Although the For-Profit Business is for profit, the book contains information that can be implemented in the NFP business.

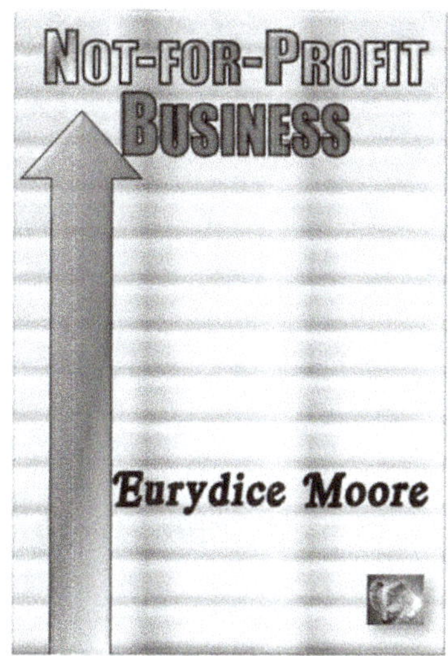


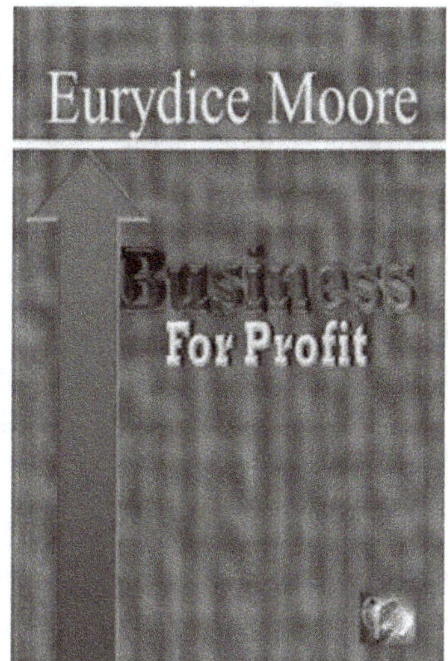


## LIFE STORY OF THE AUTHOR THAT LED TO BUSINESS VENTURE

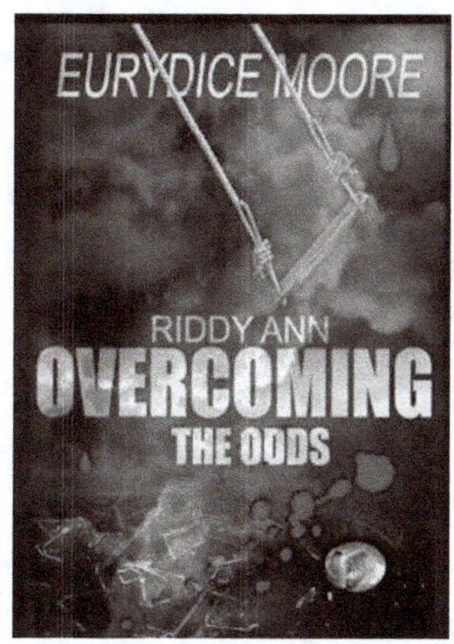